MEALS MADE
EASY

WITH

GREY POUPON® MUSTARD

*S*earching for enticing, new dishes to serve family and friends? If so, look no more. With these delectable recipes from Grey Poupon®, you can put together truly wonderful meals in just minutes. Designed to make meal preparation easier, our versatile collection takes advantage of Grey Poupon Mustards to create dishes that have outstanding flavor, but use only a few ingredients.

Creative cooks agree that Grey Poupon Mustards are more than simple spreads for sandwiches, burgers and hot dogs. They enhance the flavor of many kinds of foods with their subtle blends of herbs and spices. (The Dijon mustards even include a touch of white wine.) The appealing recipes you'll find here have been tested in both the Grey Poupon Creative Kitchens and the *Better Homes and Gardens*® Test Kitchen to ensure perfect, mouthwatering results. Once you've tried our recipes, experiment by adding a spoonful of Grey Poupon to some of your own favorite dishes. You'll be amazed at the richness and distinction it adds.

So don't hesitate. Pick up some Grey Poupon and serve one of these exceptional but easy dishes soon. Then, sit back and listen for those appreciative exclamations of "Mmmmm!"

Pictured on the Cover: Lemon-Basil Marinade (recipe, page 89)

Editorial and Design: Meredith Custom Publishing

Recipe Development: Nabisco Food Center
Better Homes and Gardens® Test Kitchen

Photography: Mike Dieter
Lyne Neymeyer

Prop Styling: Gayle Schadendorf

Food Styling: Lynn Blanchard
Jennifer Peterson

Nabisco Project Managers: Maria Feicht
Joan Francolini
Betsy Sundin

MEALS MADE EASY

WITH

GREY POUPON® MUSTARD

This seal assures you that every recipe in *Meals Made Easy with Grey Poupon® Mustard* has been tested in the *Better Homes and Gardens®* Test Kitchen. This means that each recipe is practical and reliable, and meets high standards of taste appeal.

Produced by Meredith Custom Publishing, 1912 Grand Avenue, Des Moines, IA 50309-3379. The *Better Homes and Gardens®* Test Kitchen Seal is a registered trademark of Meredith Corporation.

QUICK EVERYDAY
MEALS

No matter how busy your weeknights are, you can have these fabulous main and side dishes on the table in minutes. Whether you have to make soccer practice at 6:30 or a board meeting at 7:00, these enticing, time-saving recipes and Grey Poupon Mustards will allow you to serve delicious meals and still have time for early evening activities.

Pecan-Topped Honey Chicken (recipe, page 6);
Dijon-Glazed Carrots (recipe, page 22); Classic Dijon Vinaigrette (recipe, page 92)

PECAN-TOPPED HONEY CHICKEN

Makes 4 servings • Prep Time: 15 minutes • Cooking Time: 20 minutes

If you don't own a pastry brush, use a narrow metal spatula or the back of a spoon to spread the mustard mixture on the chicken breast halves. Pictured on pages 4–5.

4	boneless, skinless chicken breast halves (about 1 pound)
3	tablespoons GREY POUPON HONEY MUSTARD
1	teaspoon lemon juice *or* lime juice
¼	teaspoon ground cumin
½	cup chopped pecans
1	tablespoon plain dry bread crumbs
2	teaspoons margarine *or* butter, melted

❶ Rinse chicken; pat dry. In small bowl, combine mustard, lemon or lime juice and cumin. Brush mixture over both sides of chicken. Place chicken in shallow baking pan.

❷ In small bowl, combine pecans, bread crumbs and melted margarine or butter. Lightly press pecan mixture onto tops of chicken pieces. Bake at 375°F for 20 to 25 minutes or until chicken is done.

Nutrition information per serving: 258 calories, 14 g total fat (2 g saturated fat), 59 mg cholesterol, 99 mg sodium, 8 g carbohydrate, 1 g dietary fiber, 23 g protein.

CRISPY CHICKEN DIJON

Makes 4 servings • Prep Time: 15 minutes • Cooking Time: 9 minutes

For a frazzle-free weeknight meal, serve this easy entrée with buttered peas, chunky applesauce and oatmeal cookies.

4	boneless, skinless chicken breast halves (about 1 pound)
2	tablespoons all-purpose flour
¼	cup GREY POUPON DIJON, Country Dijon *or* HONEY MUSTARD
⅓	cup plain dry bread crumbs
2	tablespoons vegetable oil

❶ Rinse chicken; pat dry. Coat chicken pieces with flour, shaking off excess. Spread chicken with mustard, then roll in bread crumbs to coat evenly.

❷ In large skillet, over medium heat, cook chicken in hot oil for 4 to 5 minutes on each side or until chicken is done. (If chicken browns too quickly, reduce heat to medium low.)

Nutrition information per serving: 246 calories, 11 g total fat (2 g saturated fat), 59 mg cholesterol, 493 mg sodium, 10 g carbohydrate, 0 g dietary fiber, 24 g protein.

CREAMY CHICKEN AND MUSHROOMS

Makes 4 servings • Prep Time: 15 minutes • Cooking Time: 20 minutes

Turn this everyday dish into a sophisticated main dish by using shiitake or portobello mushrooms. Then, spoon it over elegant spinach noodles.

4	boneless, skinless chicken breast halves (about 1 pound)
2	tablespoons margarine *or* butter, divided
3	cups sliced fresh mushrooms
1	small onion, finely chopped
1	clove garlic, crushed
1½	cups whipping cream *or* heavy cream
¼	cup GREY POUPON DIJON *or* Country Dijon Mustard

❶ Rinse chicken; pat dry. In large skillet, over medium heat, cook chicken in 1 tablespoon margarine or butter for 4 to 5 minutes on each side or until chicken is done. Remove from pan; keep warm.

❷ In same skillet, cook and stir mushrooms, onion and garlic in remaining margarine until tender. Stir in whipping cream or heavy cream and mustard.

❸ Simmer gently, uncovered, over medium heat until sauce slightly thickens, stirring constantly. Return chicken to pan; heat through.

Nutrition information per serving: 519 calories, 43 g total fat (23 g saturated fat), 182 mg cholesterol, 534 mg sodium, 8 g carbohydrate, 1 g dietary fiber, 26 g protein.

CHICKEN AND BROCCOLI DIJON

CHICKEN AND BROCCOLI DIJON*

Makes 4 servings • Prep Time: 15 minutes • Cooking Time: 15 minutes

*The bold Oriental flavor of the mustard-and-soy-flavored chicken and broccoli
is especially delicious over hot cooked rice.*

1	pound boneless, skinless chicken breast halves
½	cup chicken broth
1	tablespoon soy sauce
4	cups broccoli flowerettes
1	clove garlic, crushed
1	tablespoon vegetable oil
⅓	cup GREY POUPON Country Dijon *or* DIJON MUSTARD

❶ Rinse chicken; pat dry. Cut chicken into bite-size strips. In small bowl, combine chicken broth and soy sauce; set aside.

❷ In large skillet, over medium-high heat, cook and stir broccoli and garlic in hot oil for 3 to 4 minutes or until broccoli is tender-crisp. Remove from pan; keep warm.

❸ In same skillet, cook and stir chicken strips for 3 to 4 minutes or until done. Stir in broth mixture. Heat to a boil; reduce heat. Stir in mustard. Return broccoli to pan; heat through.

Nutrition information per serving: 219 calories, 7 g total fat (2 g saturated fat), 60 mg cholesterol, 924 mg sodium,
8 g carbohydrate, 5 g dietary fiber, 27 g protein.

CRUMB-TOPPED BAKED CHICKEN BREASTS DIJON

Makes 4 servings • Prep Time: 15 minutes • Cooking Time: 20 minutes

Grey Poupon and Parmesan cheese team up with delicious results in this crispy oven-fried chicken.

- 4 boneless, skinless chicken breast halves (about 1 pound)
- 2 tablespoons GREY POUPON DIJON MUSTARD
- 1 tablespoon vinegar
- 1/4 cup plain dry bread crumbs
- 2 tablespoons grated Parmesan cheese
- 1/4 teaspoon dried thyme leaves
- 1 tablespoon margarine *or* butter, melted

❶ Rinse chicken; pat dry. Place chicken in greased shallow baking pan. In small bowl, stir together mustard and vinegar. Brush mustard mixture over chicken.

❷ In another small bowl, toss together bread crumbs, Parmesan cheese and thyme. Stir in melted margarine or butter. Lightly press crumb mixture onto tops of chicken pieces. Bake at 375°F for 20 minutes or until chicken is done.

Nutrition information per serving: 195 calories, 8 g total fat (2 g saturated fat), 62 mg cholesterol, 380 mg sodium, 5 g carbohydrate, 0 g dietary fiber, 24 g protein.

BARBECUED CHICKEN THIGHS

Makes 4 servings • Prep Time: 15 minutes • Cooking Time: 35 minutes

Having a birthday dinner for Dad? Treat him to this spunky chicken with grilled vegetable kabobs. Then, top off the meal with his favorite dessert.

- 3 tablespoons GREY POUPON HONEY MUSTARD
- 2 tablespoons cider vinegar
- 1/4 teaspoon celery seed
- 8 chicken thighs (about 2½ pounds)
- 1/2 teaspoon paprika

❶ For sauce, in small saucepan, combine mustard, vinegar and celery seed. Heat just to a boil. Remove from heat; set aside. Skin chicken thighs. Rinse chicken; pat dry. Rub paprika over surface of chicken.

❷ Grill chicken over medium heat for 35 to 40 minutes or until done, turning once halfway through cooking and basting with sauce during last 5 minutes. (Or, broil 5 to 6 inches from heat source for 28 to 32 minutes, turning once and basting with sauce during last 3 minutes.)

Nutrition information per serving: 242 calories, 11 g total fat (3 g saturated fat), 98 mg cholesterol, 104 mg sodium, 5 g carbohydrate, 0 g dietary fiber, 27 g protein.

TURKEY PASTA DIJON

Makes 4 servings • Prep Time: 15 minutes • Cooking Time: 18 minutes

Any of your favorite frozen vegetable combinations will work in this speedy pasta main dish.

8   ounces linguine
1   (16-ounce) package loose-pack frozen zucchini, carrots, cauliflower, lima beans
     and Italian green beans
1   teaspoon dried Italian seasoning
1   clove garlic, crushed
⅓   cup margarine *or* butter
2   cups chopped cooked turkey *or* chicken
⅓   cup GREY POUPON DIJON *or* Country Dijon Mustard

❶ Cook pasta according to package directions; drain. Meanwhile, in large skillet, over medium heat, cook and stir frozen vegetables, Italian seasoning and garlic in margarine or butter for 3 minutes.

❷ Stir in turkey or chicken and mustard. Cook for 1 minute more to blend flavors. Toss poultry-vegetable mixture with hot cooked pasta to coat.

Nutrition information per serving: 578 calories, 25 g total fat (5 g saturated fat), 74 mg cholesterol, 761 mg sodium,
53 g carbohydrate, 3 g dietary fiber, 33 g protein.

ASPARAGUS-SAUCED CHICKEN*

Makes 6 servings • Prep Time: 10 minutes • Cooking Time: 20 minutes

Just adding a simple garnish, such as halved orange slices, can dress up this flavorful chicken-and-rice dish.

1   (6¾-ounce) package quick-cooking long grain
    and wild rice mix *or* 1½ cups quick-cooking
    rice
6   boneless, skinless chicken breast halves *or* turkey
    breast tenderloin steaks (about 1½ pounds)
2   cups milk
1   (1.8-ounce) envelope white sauce mix

¼   cup GREY POUPON DIJON MUSTARD
1   teaspoon instant chicken bouillon granules
1   pound asparagus, trimmed and cut diagonally
    into 1½-inch pieces, *or* 1 (10-ounce) package
    frozen cut asparagus

ASPARAGUS-SAUCED CHICKEN

MENU

ASPARAGUS-SAUCED CHICKEN*

GREEN AND RED GRAPE CLUSTERS

WHOLE WHEAT ROLLS

ANGEL FOOD CAKE WITH
STRAWBERRIES

❶ Prepare rice mix or rice according to package directions. Rinse chicken or turkey; pat dry. Broil 4 to 6 inches from heat source for 10 to 15 minutes or until done, turning once halfway through cooking.

❷ Meanwhile, for sauce, in small saucepan, combine milk, white sauce mix, mustard and bouillon granules. Heat to a boil, stirring frequently. Stir in fresh or frozen asparagus. Return to a boil; reduce heat. Cook and stir for 3 to 5 minutes or until vegetables are tender-crisp.

❸ To serve, spoon asparagus sauce over chicken and rice. Garnish as desired.

Nutrition information per serving: 344 calories, 10 g total fat (3 g saturated fat), 66 mg cholesterol, 1,307 mg sodium, 33 g carbohydrate, 1 g dietary fiber, 30 g protein.

CRISPY OVEN-FRIED FISH

Makes 4 servings • Prep Time: 15 minutes • Cooking Time: 6 minutes

Buy deli coleslaw and cook up some hash brown potatoes to go along with this seafaring dish.

- 1 pound fresh haddock, orange roughy *or* cod fillets, $\frac{1}{2}$ to $\frac{3}{4}$ inch thick
- 2 tablespoons GREY POUPON DIJON *or* Country Dijon Mustard
- 2 tablespoons plain yogurt *or* dairy sour cream
- $\frac{1}{3}$ cup plain dry bread crumbs
- 2 tablespoons margarine *or* butter, melted

❶ Cut fish into 4 equal portions. Rinse fish; pat dry. In small bowl, combine mustard and yogurt or sour cream. Coat fish on all sides with mustard mixture, then roll in bread crumbs to coat evenly.

❷ Place fish on wire rack in 15$\frac{1}{2}$x10$\frac{1}{2}$x1-inch baking pan, tucking under any thin edges of fish. Drizzle fish with the melted margarine or butter.

❸ Bake at 500°F for 6 to 10 minutes or until fish flakes easily with fork.

Nutrition information per serving: 200 calories, 8 g total fat (1 g saturated fat), 60 mg cholesterol, 415 mg sodium,
7 g carbohydrate, 0 g dietary fiber, 23 g protein.

DIJON PESTO STEAK

Makes 6 servings • Prep Time: 12 minutes • Cooking Time: 12 minutes

No matter what the occasion, this special steak is a delectable way to celebrate with your family or company.
Round out the menu with your favorite rice pilaf, a spinach salad and crusty rolls.

- $\frac{1}{3}$ cup finely chopped fresh basil *or* parsley
- $\frac{1}{3}$ cup walnuts, finely chopped
- $\frac{1}{4}$ cup GREY POUPON DIJON *or* Country Dijon Mustard
- 1 clove garlic, crushed
- 1 (1$\frac{1}{2}$-pound) boneless beef sirloin *or* top round steak, cut $\frac{3}{4}$ inch thick

❶ In small bowl, combine basil or parsley, walnuts, mustard and garlic; set aside.

❷ Broil steak 6 inches from heat source for 10 to 12 minutes or to nearly desired doneness, turning once halfway through cooking. Spread top of steak with mustard mixture. Broil for 2 to 3 minutes more or until steak is desired doneness and topping is lightly browned. To serve, thinly slice diagonally across grain.

Nutrition information per serving: 258 calories, 15 g total fat (4 g saturated fat), 76 mg cholesterol, 309 mg sodium,
2 g carbohydrate, 0 g dietary fiber, 27 g protein.

BEEF AND CHUNKY TOMATO SKILLET

Makes 4 servings • Prep Time: 10 minutes • Cooking Time: 35 minutes

*If you prefer your foods with plenty of zip, make this skillet supper
with chunky Italian-style, salsa or chili tomato sauce.*

4	ounces rotini, penne *or* medium shell pasta (about 1⅓ cups)
12	ounces lean ground beef
1	medium onion, cut into thin wedges
2	cloves garlic, crushed
2	(15-ounce) cans chunky plain tomato sauce
¼	cup GREY POUPON DIJON *or* Country Dijon Mustard
½	cup pre-shredded colby *and* Monterey Jack cheese (about 2 ounces)

❶ Cook pasta according to package directions; drain. In large skillet, over medium heat, cook ground beef onion and garlic until meat is browned, stirring to break up meat; drain. Stir in tomato sauce and mustard.

❷ Heat to a boil; stir in cooked pasta. Reduce heat to medium low. Cover; cook for 4 to 5 minutes or until heated through, stirring occasionally. Remove from heat.

❸ Sprinkle cheese over beef mixture. Cover; let stand for 2 to 3 minutes or until cheese is melted.

Nutrition information per serving: 430 calories, 18 g total fat (6 g saturated fat), 67 mg cholesterol, 1,482 mg sodium, 40 g carbohydrate, 5 g dietary fiber, 27 g protein.

PORK CHOPS WITH GLAZED APPLE AND ONION; CITRUS DRESSING (RECIPE, PAGE 92)

PORK CHOPS WITH GLAZED APPLE AND ONION*

Makes 4 servings • Prep Time: 10 minutes • Cooking Time: 20 minutes

For a more colorful presentation, use two small apples—one red and one green—in place of the large apple.

4	pork loin chops, cut ¾ inch thick
2	teaspoons vegetable oil
1	medium onion, thinly sliced
1	large apple, sliced
½	cup GREY POUPON HONEY MUSTARD
¼	cup apple juice

❶ In large skillet, over medium-high heat, brown pork chops on both sides in hot oil. Reduce heat to medium; cook for 5 to 10 minutes or until chops are done. Remove to serving platter; keep warm.

❷ In same skillet, over medium-high heat, cook onion in pan drippings for 3 minutes, stirring occasionally. Stir in apple; cook for 5 minutes more or until onion and apple are tender.

❸ Stir in mustard and apple juice; heat through. Spoon sauce over chops.

Nutrition information per serving: 251 calories, 10 g total fat (3 g saturated fat), 51 mg cholesterol, 70 mg sodium, 21 g carbohydrate, 1 g dietary fiber, 16 g protein.

HONEY-RASPBERRY PORK CHOPS

Makes 4 servings • Prep Time: 10 minutes • Cooking Time: 20 minutes

Team this tasty skillet dish with a mixed greens salad, steamed yellow summer squash and rice. Complete the meal with gingerbread for dessert.

4	boneless pork loin chops, cut 1 inch thick
2	tablespoons all-purpose flour
1/3	cup GREY POUPON HONEY MUSTARD
1/4	cup seedless raspberry jam
2	tablespoons cider vinegar
1	tablespoon olive oil
1	tablespoon chopped fresh parsley

❶ Coat pork chops with flour, shaking off excess. In small bowl, combine mustard, raspberry jam and vinegar; set aside. In large skillet, over medium-high heat, brown pork chops on both sides in hot oil. Add mustard mixture.

❷ Heat to a boil; reduce heat. Cover; simmer for 10 minutes or until done. Sprinkle with parsley.

Nutrition information per serving: 273 calories, 11 g total fat (3 g saturated fat), 51 mg cholesterol, 62 mg sodium, 25 g carbohydrate, 0 g dietary fiber, 16 g protein.

PORK CHOPS WITH SWEET-SOUR MUSTARD GLAZE

Makes 6 servings • Prep Time: 10 minutes • Cooking Time: 11 minutes

Sugar snap peas, parsleyed new potatoes and brown-and-serve breadsticks are perfect partners for this hearty entrée.

1/4	cup apricot preserves
1/4	cup bottled chili sauce
2	tablespoons GREY POUPON DIJON MUSTARD
2	tablespoons water
6	boneless pork loin chops, cut 1 inch thick

❶ For glaze, cut up any large pieces of fruit in apricot preserves. In small saucepan, combine preserves, chili sauce, mustard and water. Cook and stir over medium-low heat for 5 minutes or until heated through and well blended. Remove from heat. Reserve 1/2 cup glaze until serving time.

❷ Grill or broil pork chops 3 to 4 inches from heat source for 6 to 8 minutes or until done, turning once halfway through cooking and basting with remaining glaze. To serve, spoon reserved glaze over chops.

Nutrition information per serving: 188 calories, 8 g total fat (3 g saturated fat), 51 mg cholesterol, 301 mg sodium, 12 g carbohydrate, 0 g dietary fiber, 17 g protein.

Honey Mustard Kielbasa and Potatoes

Makes 4 servings • Prep Time: 20 minutes • Cooking Time: 40 minutes

For a satisfying supper, serve this robust main dish with tomato slices, pumpernickel bread and frosty mugs of beer or lemonade.

¾ cup dry white wine, beer *or* chicken broth
⅓ cup GREY POUPON HONEY MUSTARD
2 tablespoons firmly packed light brown sugar
1 pound cooked kielbasa, cut into 1-inch pieces
4 medium potatoes, cut into ¾-inch cubes
1 large onion, sliced
Chopped fresh parsley, for garnish

In small bowl, combine wine, beer or chicken broth; mustard; and brown sugar. In large roasting pan, combine kielbasa, potatoes, onion and mustard mixture. Toss to coat well. Bake at 400°F for 40 to 50 minutes or until potatoes are tender, stirring occasionally. Garnish with parsley.

Nutrition information per serving: 641 calories, 34 g total fat (12 g saturated fat), 94 mg cholesterol, 1,094 mg sodium, 57 g carbohydrate, 2 g dietary fiber, 18 g protein.

Bean and Hash Brown Potato Skillet

Makes 4 servings • Prep Time: 10 minutes • Cooking Time: 18 minutes

When there's little time to spare in the evening, remember this easy-on-the-cook meatless recipe. It's delightful with a marinated salad from the deli and rainbow sherbet for dessert.

2 cups frozen loose-pack diced hash brown potatoes with onion and peppers, thawed
1 (10¾-ounce) can condensed cream of celery soup
¼ cup milk
3 tablespoons GREY POUPON DIJON *or* Country Dijon Mustard
½ teaspoon dried basil leaves
2 (15-ounce) cans red kidney, black *and/or* pinto beans, rinsed and drained
½ cup dairy sour cream

In large skillet, combine hash brown potatoes, celery soup, milk, mustard and basil. Cook and stir until mixture comes to a boil; reduce heat. Cover; simmer for 10 minutes. Stir in beans and sour cream; heat through.

Nutrition information per serving: 378 calories, 11 g total fat (5 g saturated fat), 22 mg cholesterol, 1,243 mg sodium, 59 g carbohydrate, 14 g dietary fiber, 19 g protein.

HAM AND SWISS PIZZA*

Makes 4 servings • Prep Time: 15 minutes • Cooking Time: 12 minutes

At your next party, cut this quick-and-easy pizza into thin wedges and serve it as an appetizer.

¾ cup red, yellow *and/or* green bell pepper cut into
 bite-size strips
1 small onion, sliced and separated into rings
2 tablespoons GREY POUPON DIJON *or*
 Country Dijon Mustard
½ teaspoon dried basil leaves
1 12-inch Italian bread shell

4 ounces diced cooked ham *or* chicken
1 cup shredded Swiss cheese *or* mozzarella cheese
 (about 4 ounces)

❶ In medium skillet, cook bell pepper strips and onion in small amount of boiling water for 2 to 3 minutes or until tender; drain. Stir in mustard and basil. Set aside.

HAM AND SWISS PIZZA

MENU

HAM AND SWISS PIZZA*

ROMAINE SALAD WITH
CHERRY TOMATOES

INSTANT BANANA PUDDING WITH
SLICED BANANAS

❷ Place bread shell on lightly greased baking sheet. Top with
bell pepper mixture and ham or chicken. Sprinkle with
Swiss cheese. Bake at 400°F for 8 to 10 minutes or until
cheese is melted and pizza is heated through.

Nutrition information per serving: 467 calories, 17 g total fat (6 g saturated fat),
46 mg cholesterol, 1,224 mg sodium, 53 g carbohydrate, 2 g dietary fiber, 28 g protein.

DIJON-GLAZED CARROTS

Makes 4 side-dish servings • Prep Time: 5 minutes • Cooking Time: 15 minutes

These zesty baby carrots are a superb serve-along for honey-baked ham or roast pork.
Pictured on pages 4–5.

- 3 cups packaged, peeled baby carrots
- 2 tablespoons margarine *or* butter
- 2 tablespoons firmly packed light brown sugar
- 2 tablespoons GREY POUPON DIJON MUSTARD
  Chopped fresh parsley, optional

❶ In covered medium saucepan, cook carrots in small amount of boiling water for 8 to 10 minutes or until tender-crisp; drain. Remove from pan; keep warm.

❷ In same saucepan, over medium heat, melt margarine or butter. Stir in brown sugar and mustard until combined. Stir in carrots. Cook and stir for 2 minutes or until carrots are glazed. Sprinkle with parsley, if desired.

Nutrition information per serving: 128 calories, 6 g total fat (1 g saturated fat), 0 mg cholesterol, 326 mg sodium,
17 g carbohydrate, 4 g dietary fiber, 2 g protein.

SAUCY MUSTARD AND BACON BEANS

Makes 4 side-dish servings • Prep Time: 10 minutes • Cooking Time: 20 minutes

Add color and pizzazz to grilled burgers or brats by
serving this three-bean combo on the side.

- 2 slices bacon, cut up
- 1 medium onion, chopped
- 1 (8-ounce) can red kidney beans, drained
- 1 (8-ounce) can lima *or* butter beans, drained
- 1 cup canned garbanzo beans
- ⅔ cup bottled barbecue sauce
- 3 tablespoons GREY POUPON HONEY MUSTARD

❶ In medium saucepan, over medium heat, cook bacon and onion until bacon is crisp and onion is tender; drain.

❷ Stir in beans, barbecue sauce and mustard. Heat to a boil; reduce heat. Cover; simmer for 10 minutes to blend flavors.

Nutrition information per serving: 204 calories, 3 g total fat (1 g saturated fat), 3 mg cholesterol, 681 mg sodium,
35 g carbohydrate, 8 g dietary fiber, 10 g protein.

Creamy Chive- and Mustard-Topped Potatoes

Makes 4 to 6 side-dish servings • Prep Time: 12 minutes • Cooking Time: 40 minutes

The dry, mealy texture of russet (sometimes labeled Idaho) potatoes makes them ideal for baking.

4   to 6 medium baking potatoes (6 to 8 ounces each)
1   (8-ounce) tub cream cheese with chives and onion
2   tablespoons GREY POUPON DIJON MUSTARD
1   tablespoon milk
¼   cup sliced pitted ripe olives

❶ Scrub potatoes; pat dry. Prick with fork. Bake at 425°F for 40 to 60 minutes or until tender.

❷ Meanwhile, in small bowl, stir together cream cheese, mustard and milk until smooth. Stir in ripe olives.

❸ Using hot pad, roll each potato gently under your hand. Using knife, cut crisscross in each top. Press in and up on ends of each potato. Top with cream cheese mixture.

Nutrition information per serving: 398 calories, 20 g total fat (10 g saturated fat), 60 mg cholesterol, 442 mg sodium,
45 g carbohydrate, 2 g dietary fiber, 9 g protein.

Lemon Dijon Pasta Toss

Makes 6 side-dish servings • Prep Time: 10 minutes • Cooking Time: 20 minutes

Easy, quick and flavorful   this lemony pasta dish will bring out the best in broiled steaks or chops.

12   ounces linguine
⅓   cup margarine *or* butter
3   tablespoons chopped fresh parsley
3   tablespoons GREY POUPON DIJON *or* Country Dijon Mustard
1   tablespoon lemon juice
2   cloves garlic, crushed
     Dash ground black pepper

Cook pasta according to package directions; drain. Meanwhile, in small saucepan, over medium heat, melt margarine or butter. Stir in parsley, mustard, lemon juice, garlic and pepper; heat through. Toss with hot cooked pasta to coat.

Nutrition information per serving: 327 calories, 12 g total fat (2 g saturated fat), 0 mg cholesterol, 311 mg sodium,
46 g carbohydrate, 0 g dietary fiber, 8 g protein.

MEDITERRANEAN COUSCOUS

MENU

DELI-ROASTED CHICKEN

MEDITERRANEAN COUSCOUS*

PITA BREAD

CANTALOUPE AND HONEYDEW MELON
CHUNKS WITH MINT

MEDITERRANEAN COUSCOUS*

Makes 6 side-dish servings • Prep Time: 15 minutes • Chilling Time: 45 minutes

Couscous is a tiny, bead-shaped product made from ground semolina that cooks quickly. Look for it with the rices and grains at the grocery store.

- 1 (10-ounce) package couscous
- ½ cup bottled Italian salad dressing
- ⅓ cup GREY POUPON DIJON *or* Country Dijon Mustard
- ½ teaspoon grated lemon peel
- 4 ounces feta cheese, crumbled
- 1 (7-ounce) jar roasted red bell peppers, drained and chopped
- ½ cup chopped pitted ripe olives

❶ Prepare couscous according to package directions; cool slightly. In small bowl, whisk together Italian salad dressing, mustard and lemon peel.

❷ In large bowl, combine feta cheese, roasted peppers and olives; stir in couscous. Pour mustard mixture over couscous mixture; toss to coat well. Cover; refrigerate for at least 45 minutes or overnight before serving. Garnish as desired.

Nutrition information per serving: 372 calories, 18 g total fat (5 g saturated fat), 17 mg cholesterol, 782 mg sodium,
42 g carbohydrate, 8 g dietary fiber, 10 g protein.

EASY WEEKEND
COOKING

After a hectic week of meals, it's nice to be able to slow the pace. In this chapter, you'll find recipes that don't take long to put together—30 minutes or less—but require a few more minutes for simmering, baking, chilling or marinating. This gives you extra time for gardening, a bicycle ride with friends or family or a chance to sit down with that bestseller you've been wanting to read.

DIJON CORN BREAD-STUFFED CHICKEN (RECIPE, PAGE 29)

QUICHE LORRAINE POUPON

Makes 4 to 6 servings • Prep Time: 15 minutes • Cooking Time: 35 minutes

*Serve this sumptuous dish with fresh fruit cups, oatmeal muffins and
orange juice spritzers for an eye-opening brunch.*

1	cup shredded Swiss cheese (about 4 ounces)
4	slices bacon, cooked and crumbled
2	tablespoons chopped green onions
1	(9-inch) unbaked pie crust
3	eggs, beaten
1	cup light cream *or* half-and-half
¼	cup GREY POUPON DIJON *or* Country Dijon Mustard

❶ Sprinkle cheese, bacon and green onions evenly over bottom of unbaked pie crust.

❷ In medium bowl, whisk together eggs, cream or half-and-half and mustard. Pour evenly over cheese mixture. Bake at 375°F for 35 to 40 minutes or until knife inserted in center comes out clean.

Nutrition information per serving: 580 calories, 40 g total fat (16 g saturated fat), 213 mg cholesterol, 759 mg sodium, 33 g carbohydrate, 1 g dietary fiber, 21 g protein.

Quiche Lorraine Florentine: Omit green onions; sprinkle 1 (10-ounce) package frozen chopped spinach, thawed and very well drained, over cheese mixture in bottom of pie crust. Continue as above.

Nutrition information per serving: 593 calories, 40 g total fat (16 g saturated fat), 213 mg cholesterol, 800 mg sodium, 35 g carbohydrate, 1 g dietary fiber, 23 g protein.

DIJON CORN BREAD-STUFFED CHICKEN

Makes 4 servings • Prep Time: 15 minutes • Cooking Time: 1¾ hours • Standing Time: 10 minutes

While the bird roasts, tuck an apple crisp dessert in the oven to bake alongside.
Pictured on pages 26–27.

1	(2½- to 3-pound) broiler-fryer chicken
1	cup sliced fresh mushrooms
4	tablespoons margarine *or* butter, divided
½	cup water
4	tablespoons GREY POUPON HONEY, DIJON *or* Country Dijon Mustard, divided
1¼	teaspoons dried thyme leaves, divided
1½	cups corn bread stuffing mix

❶ Rinse chicken; pat dry. Set aside. For stuffing, in medium saucepan, cook and stir mushrooms in 2 tablespoons margarine or butter until tender. Carefully stir in water, 3 tablespoons mustard and ¼ teaspoon thyme. Heat to a boil; remove from heat. Stir in stuffing mix. Spoon stuffing loosely into body cavity of chicken.*

❷ In small saucepan, melt remaining margarine. Stir in remaining mustard and remaining thyme. Brush herb mixture over chicken. Tie legs to tail. Twist wing tips under back. Place, breast side up, on wire rack in shallow roasting pan. Insert meat thermometer into center of an inside thigh muscle. Cover loosely with foil.

❸ Roast at 375°F for 1 hour. Remove foil. Roast for 30 to 45 minutes more or until thermometer registers 180° to 185°F. Cover chicken with foil and let stand for 10 minutes before carving.

*Note: If you like, bake the stuffing in a 1-quart casserole dish instead of inside the chicken. Bake at 375°F for 15 to 20 minutes or until heated through.

Nutrition information per serving: 488 calories, 28 g total fat (7 g saturated fat), 112 mg cholesterol, 481 mg sodium,
24 g carbohydrate, 1 g dietary fiber, 33 g protein.

Honey Mustard Teriyaki Chicken*

Makes 4 servings • Prep Time: 10 minutes • Marinating Time: 1 hour
Cooking Time: 10 minutes

*To keep all the flavorful juices inside the chicken, use tongs to turn the pieces
rather than piercing them with a fork.*

½   cup GREY POUPON HONEY MUSTARD
3   tablespoons teriyaki sauce
4   boneless, skinless chicken breast halves
    (about 1 pound)

❶ In medium bowl, combine mustard and teriyaki sauce. Reserve ⅓ cup mustard mixture for basting. Rinse chicken; pat dry. Add chicken to remaining mustard mixture, turning to coat well.

Menu

Honey Mustard Teriyaki Chicken*

Steamed sugar snap peas

Brown rice pilaf

Lettuce, cucumber and orange salad

Almond cookies

Honey Mustard Teriyaki Chicken

❷ Cover; marinate in refrigerator for 1 to 2 hours, turning the chicken occasionally.

❸ Remove chicken; discard marinade. Grill or broil chicken 4 to 6 inches from heat source for 10 to 15 minutes or until chicken is done, turning once halfway through cooking and basting frequently with the ⅓ cup reserved mustard mixture.

Nutrition information per serving: 174 calories, 3 g total fat (1 g saturated fat), 59 mg cholesterol, 464 mg sodium, 11 g carbohydrate, 0 g dietary fiber, 22 g protein.

HONEY-GLAZED CHICKEN

Makes 4 servings • Prep Time: 10 minutes • Marinating Time: 1 hour
Cooking Time: 45 minutes

Keep a zippered plastic bag in your freezer to hold chicken necks, backs, wing tips and giblets; use them later for chicken stock.

½   cup GREY POUPON HONEY MUSTARD
⅓   cup lemon juice
2   cloves garlic, crushed
1   (2½- to 3-pound) broiler-fryer chicken, cut into 8 pieces
2   tablespoons firmly packed light brown sugar

❶ In large glass baking dish, combine mustard, lemon juice and garlic; set aside. Skin chicken, if desired. Rinse chicken; pat dry.

❷ Add chicken pieces to mustard mixture, turning to coat well. Cover; marinate in refrigerator for at least 1 hour or overnight, turning chicken occasionally.

❸ Remove chicken, reserving marinade. Place chicken on wire rack in 13x9x2-inch baking pan. Pour reserved marinade over chicken; sprinkle with brown sugar. Bake at 400°F for 45 minutes or until chicken is done, basting with pan drippings.

Nutrition information per serving: 355 calories, 15 g total fat (4 g saturated fat), 99 mg cholesterol, 124 mg sodium, 19 g carbohydrate, 0 g dietary fiber, 31 g protein.

CHICKEN AND SHRIMP KABOBS

**Makes 6 servings • Prep Time: 30 minutes • Marinating Time: 2 hours
Cooking Time: 8 minutes**

*If you don't have metal skewers, use wooden ones. Soak them in water
for 30 minutes so they won't burn.*

1	pound boneless, skinless chicken breast halves
24	large fresh shrimp, peeled and deveined
1	medium zucchini, halved lengthwise and cut into 1½-inch pieces
2	small red bell peppers, cut into 1½-inch pieces
½	cup GREY POUPON HONEY MUSTARD
¼	cup reduced-sodium soy sauce
2	cloves garlic, crushed
12	(10-inch) skewers

❶ Rinse chicken; pat dry. Cut chicken into 1½-inch cubes. In large bowl, combine chicken, shrimp, zucchini and bell peppers.

❷ In small bowl, combine mustard, soy sauce and garlic. Reserve ¼ cup mustard mixture for basting. Pour remaining mustard mixture over chicken mixture, stirring to coat well. Cover; marinate in refrigerator for 2 hours, stirring occasionally.

❸ Remove chicken, shrimp and vegetables, discarding marinade. Alternately thread chicken, shrimp, zucchini and peppers onto 12 (10-inch) skewers.

❹ Grill or broil 4 to 5 inches from heat source for 8 to 10 minutes or until chicken and shrimp are done, turning occasionally and basting with reserved mustard mixture.

Nutrition information per serving: 180 calories, 3 g total fat (1 g saturated fat), 127 mg cholesterol, 509 mg sodium,
11 g carbohydrate, 0 g dietary fiber, 25 g protein.

TIP

To devein each shrimp, with a sharp knife, make a shallow slit along the back from the head end to the tail. Rinse the shrimp under cold running water, using the tip of the knife, if necessary, to help remove the vein.

SWISS CHICKEN STRATA*

Makes 6 servings • Prep Time: 15 minutes • Chilling Time: 2 hours
Cooking Time: 45 minutes • Standing Time: 10 minutes

For cooked chicken the easy way, purchase a deli-roasted chicken, remove the meat from the bones and chop it—you should get 1½ to 2 cups.

6	cups French bread cut into ½-inch cubes, divided
1½	cups shredded Gruyère *or* Swiss cheese (about 6 ounces), divided
1½	cups chopped cooked chicken *or* turkey
¾	cup chopped red *and/or* green bell pepper
4	eggs, beaten
2	cups milk
¼	cup GREY POUPON DIJON *or* Country Dijon Mustard

❶ In greased 2-quart oblong baking dish, layer 3 cups bread cubes, 1 cup cheese, the chicken or turkey and chopped bell pepper; top with remaining bread cubes.

❷ In medium bowl, whisk together eggs, milk and mustard until combined. Pour mixture over bread layer, being careful to moisten all of the bread. Sprinkle with remaining cheese. Cover; refrigerate for at least 2 hours or overnight.

❸ Bake at 325°F for 45 minutes or until knife inserted in center of bread mixture comes out clean. Let stand for 10 minutes before serving. Garnish as desired.

Nutrition information per serving: 378 calories, 18 g total fat (8 g saturated fat), 213 mg cholesterol, 645 mg sodium,
21 g carbohydrate, 0 g dietary fiber, 30 g protein.

SWISS CHICKEN STRATA

WINE-MARINATED GRILLED LAMB

Makes 12 to 14 servings • Prep Time: 15 minutes • Marinating Time: 1½ hours
Cooking Time: 1¼ hours • Standing Time: 10 minutes

Save any leftovers from this succulent grilled lamb to make gyros
or other sandwiches, salads, casseroles or soups.

1	(4- to 5-pound) boneless, butterflied leg of lamb
1	cup dry red wine
½	cup GREY POUPON DIJON *or* Country Dijon Mustard
¼	cup soy sauce
1	tablespoon chopped fresh rosemary *or* ½ teaspoon dried rosemary leaves

❶ Place lamb in large plastic bag; set in shallow dish. For marinade, in medium bowl, combine wine, mustard, soy sauce and rosemary. Pour marinade over lamb. Seal bag; marinate in refrigerator for at least 1½ hours or overnight, turning bag occasionally to help redistribute the marinade.

❷ Remove lamb, discarding marinade. If necessary to keep lamb flat during cooking, insert 2 (15-inch) metal skewers through meat at right angles, making an "X." Insert meat thermometer into lamb.

❸ In covered grill, arrange medium coals around drip pan.* Place lamb on grill rack over drip pan (not over coals); lower grill hood. Grill for 1¼ hours for medium doneness or until thermometer registers 155°F (add more coals to maintain heat as necessary). Remove skewers, if using.

❹ Cover lamb with foil and let stand for 10 minutes before carving. (The meat's temperature will rise 5° during standing.) To serve, thinly slice lamb across grain.

*Note: To roast lamb in oven, place skewered meat, fat side up, on wire rack in shallow roasting pan. Roast at 325°F for 1¼ hours for medium doneness or until thermometer registers 155°F.

Nutrition information per serving: 172 calories, 7 g total fat (2 g saturated fat), 76 mg cholesterol, 210 mg sodium,
0 g carbohydrate, 0 g dietary fiber, 25 g protein.

HONEY DIJON BARBECUE RIBETTES

Makes 8 servings • Prep Time: 10 minutes • Cooking Time: 1 hour

*This zesty barbecue sauce is so delicious, you'll want to set some aside
to brush on chops or chicken, too.*

2½	pounds pork baby back spareribs, split
2	cloves garlic, crushed
1	tablespoon vegetable oil
⅔	cup bottled chili sauce
⅔	cup GREY POUPON HONEY MUSTARD
6	thin slices lemon
½	teaspoon liquid hot pepper seasoning

❶ Place ribs in large heavy pot; add enough water to cover ribs. Over high heat, heat to a boil; reduce heat. Cover; simmer for 30 to 40 minutes or until tender. Drain.

❷ Meanwhile, for sauce, in medium saucepan, over low heat, cook garlic in hot oil until tender. Stir in chili sauce, mustard, lemon slices and hot pepper seasoning. Cook over medium heat for 2 to 3 minutes or until heated through. Remove 1 cup sauce; cover and store in refrigerator for up to 1 week.

❸ Brush ribs with some of the remaining sauce. Grill ribs over medium heat for 15 to 20 minutes or until heated through, turning frequently and basting with remaining sauce. To serve, cut ribs into serving-size pieces.

Nutrition information per serving: 252 calories, 13 g total fat (4 g saturated fat), 63 mg cholesterol, 54 mg sodium,
1 g carbohydrate, 0 g dietary fiber, 30 g protein.

Menu

ROAST PORK WITH
PINEAPPLE-MUSTARD GLAZE*

GARLIC MASHED POTATOES
(RECIPE, PAGE 82)

STEAMED GREEN BEANS

CORN BREAD MUFFINS

CHOCOLATE CAKE

ROAST PORK WITH PINEAPPLE-MUSTARD GLAZE*

Makes 6 servings • Prep Time: 10 minutes • Cooking Time: 1½ hours
Standing Time: 10 minutes

*To make carving easy, ask the butcher at your supermarket or meat market
to loosen the roast's backbone for you.*

1	(3- to 4-pound) pork loin center rib roast, backbone loosened (6 ribs)
⅓	cup apricot-pineapple preserves
¼	cup GREY POUPON HONEY MUSTARD
2	tablespoons pineapple juice *or* orange juice
1	tablespoon soy sauce
¼	teaspoon ground ginger
	Orange wedges, for garnish

❶ Place roast, rib side down, in shallow roasting pan. Insert meat thermometer into roast without touching bone. Roast at 325°F for 1½ to 2 hours or until thermometer registers 155°F.

❷ Meanwhile, for glaze, in small bowl, combine apricot-pineapple preserves, mustard, pineapple or orange juice, soy sauce and ginger. Baste roast occasionally with glaze during last 20 minutes of cooking.

❸ Cover roast with foil and let stand for 10 minutes before carving. (The meat's temperature will rise 5° during standing.) Garnish with orange wedges.

Nutrition information per serving: 273 calories, 11 g total fat (4 g saturated fat), 76 mg cholesterol, 242 mg sodium,
17 g carbohydrate, 0 g dietary fiber, 24 g protein.

ROAST PORK WITH PINEAPPLE-MUSTARD GLAZE; GARLIC MASHED POTATOES (RECIPE, PAGE 82)

CHILI- AND MUSTARD-MARINATED STEAKS

Makes 6 servings • Prep Time: 10 minutes • Marinating Time: 2 hours
Cooking Time: 8 minutes

Grilled steaks, such as these, are one of America's best-loved meals.
Don't forget to include baked potatoes and a crisp green salad.

- ½ cup GREY POUPON DIJON *or* Country Dijon Mustard
- ⅓ cup bottled chili sauce
- ⅓ cup apple juice
- ¼ teaspoon coarsely ground black pepper
- 3 (1-pound) beef T-bone steaks, cut 1 inch thick, *or* 6 (4- to 5-ounce) beef top loin steaks, cut 1 inch thick

❶ In large glass baking dish, combine mustard, chili sauce, apple juice and pepper. Add steaks, turning to coat well. Cover; marinate in refrigerator for at least 2 hours or overnight, turning occasionally.

❷ Remove steaks, discarding marinade. Grill or broil steaks 3 to 4 inches from heat source for 5 minutes. Turn and grill to desired doneness; allow 3 to 7 minutes more for medium-rare or 7 to 10 minutes more for medium.

❸ To serve T-bone steaks, if using, cut the steaks in half.

Nutrition information per serving: 238 calories, 11 g total fat (4 g saturated fat), 80 mg cholesterol, 408 mg sodium,
3 g carbohydrate, 0 g dietary fiber, 29 g protein.

BEEF POT ROAST

Makes 4 to 6 servings • Prep Time: 10 minutes • Cooking Time: 2 hours 35 minutes

While this home-style roast simmers, toss together a spinach and mandarin orange salad to serve with your favorite vinaigrette.

1   (2½-pound) beef bottom round roast
2   tablespoons all-purpose flour
1   tablespoon vegetable oil
1   (14½-ounce) can beef broth
⅔   cup GREY POUPON DIJON MUSTARD
1   (20-ounce) package frozen stew vegetables

Coat roast with flour, shaking off excess. In large heavy pot, over medium heat, brown roast on all sides in hot oil. Add beef broth. Heat to a boil; reduce heat. Cover; simmer for 2 hours. Stir in mustard. Add frozen vegetables; return to a simmer. Cover; simmer for 20 minutes more or until roast and vegetables are tender.

Nutrition information per serving: 614 calories, 26 g total fat (8 g saturated fat), 193 mg cholesterol, 1,517 mg sodium, 20 g carbohydrate, 2 g dietary fiber, 69 g protein.

SAVORY BEEF STEW

Makes 4 to 6 servings • Prep Time: 20 minutes • Cooking Time: 1 hour 40 minutes

Gather the family together on a Saturday night for a meal of this hearty stew; lettuce wedges with salad dressing, Italian bread and brownies.

1½   pounds beef stew meat, cut into 1-inch cubes
2   tablespoons all-purpose flour
2   tablespoons vegetable oil
2   medium onions, sliced
1   (14½-ounce) can beef broth
1   (10-ounce) package frozen mixed vegetables
⅓   cup GREY POUPON DIJON MUSTARD

❶ Coat beef cubes with flour, shaking off excess. In large heavy pot, over medium-high heat, brown meat, half at a time, in hot oil. Return all meat to pan.

❷ Add onions and beef broth. Heat to a boil; reduce heat. Cover; simmer for 45 minutes. Stir in frozen vegetables; return to a simmer. Simmer, uncovered, for 30 minutes more or until meat is tender. Stir in mustard; heat through.

Nutrition information per serving: 442 calories, 21 g total fat (6 g saturated fat), 124 mg cholesterol, 944 mg sodium, 16 g carbohydrate, 1 g dietary fiber, 46 g protein.

PEANUT CHICKEN SKEWERS*

**Makes 12 appetizers • Prep Time: 20 minutes • Marinating Time: 1 hour
Cooking Time: 4 minutes**

*Based on Indonesian satay, this flavorful appetizer features marinated meat grilled
or broiled on skewers and served with a spicy peanut dipping sauce.*

¾ cup GREY POUPON HONEY MUSTARD
⅓ cup chunky peanut butter
2 tablespoons soy sauce
1 clove garlic, crushed
1 pound boneless, skinless chicken breast halves

12 (6-inch) wooden skewers
1 tablespoon water

❶ In medium bowl, combine mustard, peanut butter, soy
sauce and garlic. Reserve ½ cup mustard mixture until
serving time. Rinse chicken; pat dry. Cut chicken into

PEANUT CHICKEN SKEWERS

MENU

PEANUT CHICKEN SKEWERS*

MUSTARD-AND-BEER CHEESE DIP
(RECIPE, PAGE 93)

YOGURT DIP WITH ASSORTED
CUT-UP FRUIT

CHEESE POPCORN

¼-inch-thick strips. Add chicken strips to remaining mustard mixture, stirring to coat well. Cover; marinate in refrigerator for at least 1 hour or overnight, stirring the mixture occasionally.

❷ Soak wooden skewers in enough water to cover for at least 1 hour; drain.

❸ Remove chicken; discard marinade. Thread chicken strips onto wooden skewers, accordion fashion. Grill or broil chicken 4 to 6 inches from heat source for 4 minutes or until chicken is done, turning once halfway through cooking. Blend the 1 tablespoon water into reserved ½ cup mustard mixture.

❹ To serve, arrange skewers on serving platter. Garnish as desired. Serve reserved mustard mixture as a dipping sauce with chicken.

Nutrition information per appetizer: 96 calories, 4 g total fat (1 g saturated fat), 20 mg cholesterol, 183 mg sodium, 6 g carbohydrate, 0 g dietary fiber, 9 g protein.

ORANGE DIJON CHICKEN WINGS

Makes 24 appetizers • Prep Time: 15 minutes • Marinating Time: 1 hour
Cooking Time: 8 minutes

Everyone will enjoy the tangy, sweet flavor of this tongue-tingling glaze.

12	chicken wings
½	cup GREY POUPON Country Dijon Mustard
½	cup ketchup
⅓	cup orange marmalade
1	tablespoon dried minced onion
1	tablespoon reduced-sodium soy sauce
1	clove garlic, crushed

❶ Rinse chicken; pat dry. Cut off and discard wing tips. Cut each wing at joint to make 2 sections. Place chicken in plastic bag; set in shallow dish. In small bowl, blend mustard, ketchup, orange marmalade, minced onion, soy sauce and garlic.

❷ Pour ½ cup mustard mixture over chicken. Seal bag; marinate in refrigerator for at least 1 hour or overnight, turning bag occasionally. Cover; refrigerate remaining mustard mixture until serving time.

❸ Remove chicken wings, discarding marinade. Place chicken on greased unheated rack of broiler pan. Broil 4 to 6 inches from heat source for 8 to 10 minutes or until done, turning occasionally. In small saucepan, heat reserved mustard mixture to a boil. Serve as a dipping sauce with chicken wings.

Nutrition information per appetizer: 71 calories, 3 g total fat (1 g saturated fat), 15 mg cholesterol, 206 mg sodium,
4 g carbohydrate, 0 g dietary fiber, 5 g protein.

ROASTED POTATOES POUPON

Makes 6 side-dish servings • Prep Time: 15 minutes • Cooking Time: 45 minutes

*Stirring the potatoes halfway through the roasting time ensures
that they'll brown and crisp up evenly.*

½ cup GREY POUPON DIJON, HONEY *or* Country Dijon Mustard
½ cup olive oil
3 pounds baking potatoes, cut into 1½-inch cubes
2 medium onions, sliced
   Chopped fresh parsley, for garnish

❶ In small bowl, combine mustard and oil. In large bowl, combine potatoes, onions and mustard mixture; toss to coat well.

❷ Spread in 15½x10½x1-inch baking pan. Bake at 400°F for 45 to 50 minutes or until potatoes are tender and crispy, stirring once. Garnish with parsley.

Nutrition information per serving: 429 calories, 20 g total fat (2 g saturated fat), 0 mg cholesterol, 523 mg sodium,
57 g carbohydrate, 2 g dietary fiber, 7 g protein.

SAVORY SAUCEPAN STUFFING

**Makes 4 side-dish servings • Prep Time: 15 minutes • Cooking Time: 15 minutes
Standing Time: 5 minutes**

Team this herb-seasoned stuffing, cooked on the stovetop, with roast or grilled pork or chicken.

1   cup coarsely chopped fresh mushrooms
1   medium onion, chopped
¼ cup margarine *or* butter
1¾ cups water
¼ cup GREY POUPON Country Dijon Mustard
4   cups herb-seasoned stuffing croutons
2   tablespoons chopped fresh parsley

❶ In large saucepan, over medium-high heat, cook and stir mushrooms and onion in margarine or butter until tender. Stir in water and mustard. Heat to a boil; reduce heat. Cover; simmer for 5 minutes. Remove from heat.

❷ Add stuffing croutons and parsley, stirring to coat well. Cover; let stand for 5 minutes. Fluff with fork before serving.

Nutrition information per serving: 459 calories, 15 g total fat (2 g saturated fat), 0 mg cholesterol, 1,638 mg sodium,
69 g carbohydrate, 1 g dietary fiber, 10 g protein.

DINNERTIME
SALADS

Look no further for an appealing array of fresh, flavorful main- and side-dish salads. A cut above the ordinary mound of iceberg lettuce, these recipes turn an imaginative combination of ingredients, such as asparagus, broccoli, mandarin oranges or apples with, of course, Grey Poupon Mustards, into incredible salads with extraordinary color, texture and taste.

WARM DILLED CHICKEN AND POTATO SALAD (RECIPE, PAGE 48)

WARM DILLED CHICKEN AND POTATO SALAD

Makes 4 servings • Prep Time: 15 minutes • Cooking Time: 25 minutes

When juicy summer tomatoes are at their peak, serve this flavor-packed salad in tomato cups. Pictured on pages 46–47.

1	pound small red-skinned potatoes, quartered
½	cup bottled peppercorn ranch salad dressing
2	tablespoons chopped fresh dill
2	tablespoons GREY POUPON DIJON *or* Country Dijon Mustard
12	ounces boneless, skinless chicken breast halves
1	tablespoon olive oil *or* vegetable oil
1½	cups chopped red, yellow *and/or* green bell pepper

❶ In covered large saucepan, cook potatoes in boiling water for 15 minutes or until tender; drain.

❷ Meanwhile, for dressing, in small bowl, combine peppercorn ranch salad dressing, dill and mustard.

❸ Rinse chicken; pat dry. Cut into bite-size strips. In large skillet, over medium-high heat, cook and stir chicken in hot oil for 3 to 4 minutes or until done.

❹ In large bowl, combine cooked chicken, cooked potatoes and chopped bell pepper. Pour dressing over potato mixture; toss gently to coat salad ingredients with dressing.

Nutrition information per serving: 358 calories, 18 g total fat (3 g saturated fat), 52 mg cholesterol, 432 mg sodium, 29 g carbohydrate, 1 g dietary fiber, 20 g protein.

HONEY CHICKEN SALAD POUPON

Makes 4 servings • Prep Time: 20 minutes • Cooking Time: 15 minutes

For a special warm-weather luncheon, spoon this easy chicken salad over cantaloupe wedges and serve it with blueberry muffins. End the meal with white chocolate cheesecake for dessert.

½	cup mayonnaise
⅓	cup GREY POUPON HONEY MUSTARD
1	tablespoon red wine vinegar
1½	pounds boneless, skinless chicken breast halves, cooked and cubed
2	stalks celery, sliced
¼	cup chopped red onion
8	(7- to 8-inch) flour tortillas, warmed

❶ For dressing, in small bowl, combine mayonnaise, mustard and vinegar.

❷ In medium bowl, combine chicken, celery and red onion. Pour dressing over chicken mixture; toss gently to coat. Cover; refrigerate until serving time.

❸ To serve, spoon chicken mixture onto tortillas; roll up.

Nutrition information per serving: 606 calories, 31 g total fat (6 g saturated fat), 105 mg cholesterol, 524 mg sodium, 40 g carbohydrate, 2 g dietary fiber, 37 g protein.

LEMON GRILLED CHICKEN AND PASTA SALAD*

Makes 6 servings • Prep Time: 15 minutes • Cooking Time: 35 minutes • Chilling Time: 1 hour

This tangy pasta salad is great for picnics. Chill the salad thoroughly, then pack it on ice and tote it along to your favorite park.

½   cup GREY POUPON DIJON MUSTARD
⅓   cup olive oil
¼   cup lemon juice
10   ounces bow-tie pasta (about 4½ cups), cooked and drained

1   pound boneless, skinless chicken breast halves, grilled and sliced
2   cups broccoli flowerettes, cooked tender-crisp and drained
1   medium red bell pepper, coarsely chopped

LEMON GRILLED CHICKEN AND PASTA SALAD

MENU

LEMON GRILLED CHICKEN
AND PASTA SALAD*

CRISP BREADSTICKS

SLICED TOMATOES

FRESH BERRIES WITH
WHIPPED CREAM

❶ For dressing, in small bowl, whisk together mustard, oil and lemon juice. In large bowl, combine cooked pasta, chicken, broccoli and bell pepper.

❷ Pour dressing over pasta mixture; toss gently to coat. Cover; refrigerate the salad for at least 1 hour or overnight before serving.

Nutrition information per serving: 395 calories, 17 g total fat (3 g saturated fat),
80 mg cholesterol, 561 mg sodium, 36 g carbohydrate, 2 g dietary fiber, 23 g protein.

Dijon Asparagus Pasta Salad

Makes 4 servings • Prep Time: 15 minutes • Cooking Time: 20 minutes
Chilling Time: 2 hours

This sophisticated salad also makes a sensational brown bag lunch. Carry it to work along with an ice pack in an insulated lunch box.

4	ounces linguine, broken in half
1	pound asparagus, trimmed and cut diagonally into 1½-inch pieces, *or* 1 (10-ounce) package frozen cut asparagus
½	cup halved cherry tomatoes
½	cup cubed cheddar *or* mozzarella cheese (about 2 ounces)
½	cup bottled poppy seed salad dressing *or* coleslaw salad dressing
3	to 4 tablespoons GREY POUPON DIJON *or* Country Dijon Mustard
⅓	cup pine nuts *or* slivered almonds, toasted

❶ In large saucepan, cook linguine in lightly salted boiling water for 5 minutes. Add fresh or frozen asparagus; return to a boil. Cook for 3 to 4 minutes more or until linguine is tender but still slightly firm and asparagus is tender-crisp; drain. Rinse with cold water; drain again. Transfer to large bowl. Add cherry tomatoes and cheese; toss gently.

❷ For dressing, in small bowl, combine poppy seed or coleslaw salad dressing and mustard. Pour dressing over pasta mixture; toss gently to coat. Cover; refrigerate for at least 2 hours or overnight.

❸ If salad seems less creamy after chilling, stir in a small amount (1 to 3 tablespoons) of milk before serving. Sprinkle with pine nuts or almonds.

Nutrition information per serving: 414 calories, 25 g total fat (6 g saturated fat), 35 mg cholesterol, 777 mg sodium, 38 g carbohydrate, 2 g dietary fiber, 13 g protein.

Easy Pasta Salad Dijon

Makes 6 servings • Prep Time: 20 minutes
Cooking Time: 18 minutes • Chilling Time: 2 hours

The tri-colored pasta makes this salad as festive as it is delicious. If you can't find it at your local supermarket, use plain rotini instead.

12	ounces tri-colored rotini pasta (about 5 cups)
2	medium carrots, sliced
2	small red bell peppers, chopped
¾	cup diced deli salami (about 4 ounces)
¾	cup diced provolone cheese (about 3 ounces)
¾	cup bottled Italian salad dressing
½	cup GREY POUPON Country Dijon *or* DIJON MUSTARD

❶ In large saucepan, cook pasta in lightly salted boiling water for 4 minutes. Add carrots and bell peppers; return to a boil. Cook for 4 to 5 minutes more or until pasta is tender but still slightly firm and vegetables are tender-crisp; drain. Rinse with cold water; drain again. Transfer to large bowl. Add salami and cheese; toss gently.

❷ For dressing, in small bowl, whisk together Italian salad dressing and mustard. Reserve ¼ cup dressing. Cover; refrigerate until serving time.

❸ Pour remaining dressing over pasta mixture; toss gently to coat. Cover; refrigerate for at least 2 hours or overnight before serving.

❹ To serve, pour reserved dressing over pasta mixture; toss gently to coat.

Nutrition information per serving: 497 calories, 25 g total fat (7 g saturated fat), 25 mg cholesterol, 1,287 mg sodium, 48 g carbohydrate, 3 g dietary fiber, 15 g protein.

GRILLED BEEF AND BEAN SALAD WITH TOMATOES

MENU

GRILLED BEEF AND BEAN SALAD
WITH TOMATOES*

GARLIC TOAST

RASPBERRY SHERBET WITH
SUGAR COOKIES

GRILLED BEEF AND BEAN SALAD WITH TOMATOES*

Makes 4 to 6 servings • Prep Time: 20 minutes • Cooking Time: 8 minutes

*When you don't have the time to grill steak, substitute cooked beef
from the deli in this inviting salad.*

½	cup bottled ranch salad dressing
⅓	cup GREY POUPON DIJON MUSTARD
	Leaf lettuce leaves
1	pound beef top round steak, grilled and thinly sliced
1	pound green beans, trimmed, cooked tender-crisp and drained
6	plum tomatoes, sliced

❶ For dressing, in small bowl, combine ranch salad dressing and mustard. Cover; refrigerate until serving time.

❷ To serve, arrange lettuce leaves, beef slices, green beans and tomatoes on 4 to 6 dinner plates. Drizzle each salad with some of the dressing.

Nutrition information per serving: 356 calories, 19 g total fat (3 g saturated fat), 80 mg cholesterol, 762 mg sodium,
15 g carbohydrate, 4 g dietary fiber, 32 g protein.

SHRIMP AND SPINACH SALAD

SHRIMP AND SPINACH SALAD*

Makes 4 servings • Prep Time: 30 minutes • Cooking Time: 8 minutes

The next time you're entertaining on a weeknight, consider serving this eye-catching salad. You can cook and chill the shrimp the night before, or pick up cooked shrimp at a local seafood market.

- 1 (11-ounce) can mandarin oranges
- ½ cup dairy sour cream
- ¼ cup GREY POUPON HONEY MUSTARD
- 6 cups torn spinach (about ½ of a [16-ounce] package)
- 1 pound large fresh shrimp, cooked, peeled and deveined
- ½ cup thinly sliced red onion
  Sliced almonds, toasted, for garnish

❶ Drain mandarin oranges, reserving 2 tablespoons liquid. Cover; refrigerate oranges. For dressing, in small bowl, combine sour cream, mustard and reserved mandarin orange liquid. Cover; refrigerate until serving time.

❷ To serve, arrange spinach, shrimp, onion and mandarin oranges on 4 dinner plates. Drizzle each salad with dressing. Garnish with almonds.

Nutrition information per serving: 219 calories, 7 g total fat (4 g saturated fat), 143 mg cholesterol, 252 mg sodium,
21 g carbohydrate, 3 g dietary fiber, 18 g protein.

Warm Scallop and Spinach Salad

Makes 4 servings • Prep Time: 15 minutes • Cooking Time: 5 minutes

*For an exceptional meal, complement this seafood salad with soft breadsticks
and glasses of dry white wine or sparkling water.*

6	cups torn spinach (about ½ of a [16-ounce] package)
1	large red bell pepper, cut into thin strips
3	tablespoons GREY POUPON HONEY MUSTARD
2	tablespoons water
2	tablespoons lemon juice
12	ounces fresh *or* frozen bay scallops, thawed and drained
2	tablespoons vegetable oil

❶ In large bowl, combine spinach and bell pepper. For dressing, in screw-top jar, combine mustard, water and lemon juice. Cover; shake well. Set aside.

❷ In large skillet, over medium-high heat, cook and stir scallops in hot oil for 1 to 3 minutes or until scallops are opaque. Remove scallops with slotted spoon, reserving drippings in skillet. Add scallops to spinach mixture.

❸ Shake dressing again; add to drippings in skillet. Heat just to a boil. Pour hot dressing over spinach mixture; toss gently to coat. Serve immediately.

Nutrition information per serving: 164 calories, 8 g total fat (1 g saturated fat), 25 mg cholesterol, 205 mg sodium,
11 g carbohydrate, 2 g dietary fiber, 14 g protein.

POACHED SALMON AND GREENS WITH LEMON MUSTARD DRESSING

Makes 4 servings • Prep Time: 20 minutes

To poach the salmon fillets, in a large skillet, heat 1½ cups water to a boil. Add salmon. Return to a boil; reduce heat. Cover; simmer for 4 to 6 minutes per ½-inch thickness of fish.

- ¼ cup GREY POUPON DIJON MUSTARD
- 1 tablespoon lemon juice
- ¼ cup dairy sour cream
- ¼ cup vegetable oil
- 1½ teaspoons chopped fresh dill *or* ½ teaspoon dried dillweed
- 8 cups torn mixed salad greens (about 1 [10-ounce] package)
- 8 ounces fresh salmon fillets, poached, skinned and flaked

❶ For dressing, in small bowl, combine mustard and lemon juice. Slowly stir in sour cream and oil. Stir in dill. Cover; refrigerate the dressing until serving time.

❷ To serve, on large serving platter, arrange salad greens and salmon. Drizzle salad with dressing.

Nutrition information per serving: 237 calories, 20 g total fat (4 g saturated fat), 17 mg cholesterol, 430 mg sodium, 4 g carbohydrate, 1 g dietary fiber, 11 g protein.

MEXICAN MARKET SALAD

Make 6 side-dish servings • Prep Time: 15 minutes • Chilling Time: 1 hour

Feature this south-of-the-border vegetable salad served in purchased tortilla bowls with grilled chicken and frozen margaritas or ice water with lime wedges.

- ¼ cup bottled Italian salad dressing
- ¼ cup GREY POUPON HONEY MUSTARD
- 1 teaspoon chili powder
- 2 (15¼-ounce) cans whole kernel corn, drained
- 2 ripe large tomatoes, chopped
- 1 medium green bell pepper, cut into strips
- 1 medium red onion, halved lengthwise and sliced

❶ For dressing, in small bowl, whisk together Italian salad dressing, mustard and chili powder. In large bowl, combine corn, tomatoes, bell pepper and onion.

❷ Pour dressing over corn mixture; toss gently to coat. Cover; refrigerate for at least 1 hour or overnight before serving.

Nutrition information per serving: 169 calories, 6 g total fat (1 g saturated fat), 0 mg cholesterol, 409 mg sodium, 29 g carbohydrate, 3 g dietary fiber, 3 g protein.

TOMATO-MOZZARELLA SALAD DIJON*

Makes 4 side-dish servings • Prep Time: 15 minutes

The flavor of fresh basil makes this summertime salad truly distinctive.

⅓ cup olive oil
¼ cup GREY POUPON Country Dijon *or*
    DIJON MUSTARD
2 tablespoons lemon juice
4 ripe medium tomatoes, sliced
8 ounces mozzarella cheese, sliced

1 small red onion, cut into slivers
1 tablespoon small fresh basil leaves *or* chopped
    fresh basil

❶ For dressing, in small bowl, whisk together oil, mustard
and lemon juice. Cover; refrigerate until serving time.

TOMATO-MOZZARELLA SALAD DIJON

MENU

GRILLED BURGERS

TOMATO-MOZZARELLA SALAD DIJON*

CORN ON THE COB

CARROT AND CELERY STICKS

BLUEBERRY PIE WITH VANILLA
ICE CREAM

❷ To serve, arrange tomato and cheese slices on 4 salad
plates. Drizzle each serving with dressing. Sprinkle with
onion and basil.

Nutrition information per serving: 350 calories, 27 g total fat (8 g saturated fat),
32 mg cholesterol, 635 mg sodium, 9 g carbohydrate, 2 g dietary fiber, 15 g protein.

Roasted Potato and Bean Salad

Makes 6 servings • Prep Time: 20 minutes • Cooking Time: 25 minutes

Give this colorful salad even more Italian flair by replacing the bacon with chopped pepperoni.

½ cup GREY POUPON DIJON *or* HONEY MUSTARD
½ cup bottled hearty Italian salad dressing
2 pounds red-skinned potatoes, cut into 1-inch cubes
1 (15-ounce) can garbanzo beans, rinsed and drained
1 large green *or* red bell pepper, chopped
10 slices bacon, cooked and crumbled
3 green onions, sliced

❶ For dressing, in small bowl, whisk together mustard and Italian salad dressing. In medium bowl, pour ¼ cup dressing over potatoes; toss to coat well. Arrange potatoes in lightly greased 15½x10½x1-inch baking pan. Bake at 425°F for 20 to 25 minutes or until potatoes are tender.

❷ Meanwhile, in large bowl, combine garbanzo beans, bell pepper, bacon and green onions. Pour remaining dressing over bean mixture; toss to coat well. Gently stir in roasted potatoes. Serve warm.

Nutrition information per serving: 394 calories, 17 g total fat (3 g saturated fat), 9 mg cholesterol, 1,046 mg sodium, 50 g carbohydrate, 4 g dietary fiber, 11 g protein.

Red-Skinned Potato Salad with Dijon Dressing

Makes 6 side-dish servings • Prep Time: 15 minutes
Cooking Time: 25 minutes • Chilling Time: 1 hour

Perk up grilled chicken breast sandwiches with this zesty side dish.

⅓ cup GREY POUPON DIJON *or* Country Dijon Mustard
¼ cup dairy sour cream
¼ cup mayonnaise
2 pounds small red-skinned potatoes, cooked and quartered
1 large tomato, seeded and chopped
4 slices bacon, cooked and crumbled
1 tablespoon chopped green onion

❶ In large bowl, blend mustard, sour cream and mayonnaise. Gently stir in potatoes, tomato, bacon and green onion.

❷ Cover; refrigerate for at least 1 hour or overnight before serving.

Nutrition information per serving: 279 calories, 13 g total fat (3 g saturated fat), 13 mg cholesterol, 474 mg sodium, 36 g carbohydrate, 2 g dietary fiber, 6 g protein.

Red Leaf Salad with Honey Vinaigrette

Makes 4 side-dish servings • Prep Time: 15 minutes

Salad and soup are the perfect pair for feeding hungry family or friends, especially if you choose a hearty bean or lentil soup and this refreshing fruit-and-greens salad. Featured in the menu on page 34.

4	cups torn red leaf lettuce
1	orange, peeled, halved lengthwise and sliced
1	apple, cored and cut into bite-size pieces
½	of a small cucumber, thinly sliced
3	tablespoons sugar
3	tablespoons white wine vinegar
2	tablespoons GREY POUPON HONEY MUSTARD

❶ Divide lettuce among 4 salad plates. Top each serving with orange, apple and cucumber.

❷ For dressing, in screw-top jar, combine sugar, vinegar and mustard. Cover; shake well. Drizzle each salad with dressing.

Nutrition information per serving: 95 calories, 0 g total fat (0 g saturated fat), 0 mg cholesterol, 13 mg sodium,
23 g carbohydrate, 2 g dietary fiber, 1 g protein.

Red Cabbage Slaw

Makes 6 side-dish servings • Prep Time: 20 minutes

To toast the pecans for this tempting salad, place them in a small skillet. Over medium heat, cook and stir the nuts for 5 to 7 minutes or until golden.

2	cups shredded red cabbage
2	cups shredded carrots
1	medium apple, peeled and chopped
½	cup pecan pieces, toasted
¼	cup vegetable oil
3	tablespoons GREY POUPON HONEY MUSTARD
2	tablespoons cider vinegar

❶ In large bowl, combine cabbage, carrots, apple and pecans. For dressing, in screw-top jar, combine oil, mustard and vinegar. Cover; shake well.

❷ Pour dressing over cabbage mixture; toss to coat well. Serve immediately or cover and refrigerate for up to 2 hours.

Nutrition information per serving: 190 calories, 15 g total fat (2 g saturated fat), 0 mg cholesterol, 26 mg sodium,
13 g carbohydrate, 3 g dietary fiber, 1 g protein.

CASUAL GET-TOGETHERS

If a celebration is in order and company is on the way, these easy-on-the-cook recipes are sure to please both you and your guests. For any type of gathering—from a going-away party to a baby shower to an after-the-game supper—you can perk up the festivities with these uncomplicated ideas that will win you rave reviews.

HONEY MUSTARD BRIE AMANDINE (RECIPE, PAGE 66)

Honey Mustard Brie Amandine

Makes 8 appetizer servings • Prep Time: 15 minutes • Cooking Time: 20 minutes
Standing Time: 10 minutes

To be sure the edges of the pastry stay sealed, brush them with water before you press them together.
Pictured on pages 64–65.

½   of a (17¼-ounce) package frozen puff pastry (1 sheet), thawed
1   (8-ounce) wheel of Brie cheese
2   tablespoons GREY POUPON HONEY MUSTARD
⅓   cup sliced almonds, toasted
1   egg, beaten
     Apple wedges, grapes *and/or* assorted crackers

❶ On floured surface, roll pastry to flatten slightly. Brush top and sides of cheese wheel with mustard; coat with almonds. Place, top side down, in center of pastry sheet. Gently fold pastry around cheese, trimming as necessary so pastry just overlaps at the edges. Seal edges. Place, seam side down, on greased baking sheet. Decorate with cutouts from pastry trimmings. Brush with beaten egg.

❷ Bake at 400°F for 15 to 18 minutes or until golden. Let stand for 10 minutes before serving. Serve with apples, grapes and/or assorted crackers.

Nutrition information per serving of Brie appetizer: 274 calories, 20 g total fat (5 g saturated fat), 55 mg cholesterol, 304 mg sodium,
13 g carbohydrate, 0 g dietary fiber, 9 g protein.

Ham and Gouda Quesadilla Snacks

Makes 24 appetizers • Prep Time: 20 minutes • Cooking Time: 16 minutes

1½   cups shredded smoked Gouda cheese (about 6 ounces)
1   cup chopped cooked ham
½   cup pitted ripe olives, chopped
¼   cup minced red onion
½   cup GREY POUPON Country Dijon Mustard
8   (6- or 7-inch) flour tortillas
      Dairy sour cream, optional

In medium bowl, combine cheese, ham, olives and onion. Spread 1 tablespoon mustard on each flour tortilla. Spread about ⅓ cup cheese mixture over half of each tortilla. Fold tortillas in half to cover filling. In large nonstick skillet, over medium heat, cook tortillas in batches for 4 minutes or until tortillas are crisp and filling is heated through, turning once. Cut each into 3 wedges; arrange on serving platter. Serve warm with sour cream, if desired.

Nutrition information per appetizer: 65 calories, 3 g total fat (2 g saturated fat), 11 mg cholesterol, 292 mg sodium,
4 g carbohydrate, 0 g dietary fiber, 4 g protein.

SPIRAL REUBEN DIJON BITES

Makes 32 appetizers • Prep Time: 20 minutes • Cooking Time: 10 minutes

Save some time on the day of the party by preparing these delicious morsels ahead and freezing them.

- ½ of a (17¼-ounce) package frozen puff pastry (1 sheet), thawed
- ¼ cup GREY POUPON DIJON MUSTARD
- ¾ cup shredded Swiss cheese (about 3 ounces)
- 6 to 8 slices deli corned beef (about 6 ounces)
- 1 egg, beaten
- 1 tablespoon caraway seed
  Additional GREY POUPON DIJON MUSTARD

❶ On floured surface, roll pastry to 12x10-inch rectangle. Spread ¼ cup mustard evenly over pastry; top with cheese, then corned beef. Cut crosswise in half. Roll up each rectangle from short end, jelly-roll fashion; seal seams.*

❷ Cut each roll into 16 slices. Place, cut sides up, on lightly greased baking sheets. Brush with beaten egg and sprinkle with caraway seed. Bake at 400°F for 10 to 12 minutes or until golden. Serve warm with additional mustard.

*Note: If you like, you may prepare the rolls ahead to this point, then wrap and freeze. To serve, thaw at room temperature for 30 minutes. Slice and bake as above.

Nutrition information per appetizer: 57 calories, 4 g total fat (1 g saturated fat), 12 mg cholesterol, 135 mg sodium,
3 g carbohydrate, 0 g dietary fiber, 3 g protein.

BARBECUE-STYLE CHICKEN WINGS

Makes 16 appetizers • Prep Time: 10 minutes • Cooking Time: 40 minutes

The spiciness of this party-starter will depend on the firepower of the barbecue sauce you use.

- 8 chicken wings
- ½ cup bottled barbecue sauce
- ¼ cup GREY POUPON HONEY MUSTARD

Rinse chicken; pat dry. Cut off and discard wing tips. Cut each wing at joint to make 2 sections. Place chicken in shallow baking pan. Bake at 375°F for 30 minutes; drain. Meanwhile, in small bowl, blend barbecue sauce and mustard. Brush chicken with mustard mixture. Bake for 10 minutes more or until done.

Nutrition information per appetizer: 63 calories, 4 g total fat (1 g saturated fat), 14 mg cholesterol, 81 mg sodium,
3 g carbohydrate, 0 g dietary fiber, 5 g protein.

TOMATO BRUSCHETTA DIJON

Tomato Bruschetta Dijon*

Makes about 32 appetizers • Prep Time: 25 minutes • Chilling Time: 30 minutes

*A French baguette is crisp and golden on the outside and chewy
on the inside, making it perfect for this appetizer.*

2	tablespoons GREY POUPON DIJON MUSTARD
2	tablespoons olive oil
1	tablespoon red wine vinegar
2	cups chopped tomatoes
½	cup sliced green onions
½	cup sliced pitted ripe olives
	Baguette-style French bread, sliced and lightly toasted

❶ In small bowl, blend mustard, oil and vinegar. In medium bowl, combine tomatoes, green onions and olives. Pour mustard mixture over tomato mixture; toss to coat.

❷ Cover; refrigerate for at least 30 minutes or overnight to blend flavors.

❸ To serve, spoon about 1 tablespoon tomato mixture onto each toasted baguette slice. Garnish as desired.

Nutrition information per appetizer: 34 calories, 2 g total fat (0 g saturated fat), 0 mg cholesterol, 78 mg sodium,
4 g carbohydrate, 0 g dietary fiber, 1 g protein.

Hot Crab Dip

Makes about 1½ cups (enough for 8 appetizer servings) • Prep Time: 10 minutes
Cooking Time: 15 minutes

For a change of pace, serve this tasty seafood dip with pieces of pumpernickel or whole wheat bread.

1	(6-ounce) can crabmeat, drained, flaked and cartilage removed
4	ounces cream cheese, softened
¼	cup thinly sliced green onions
¼	cup mayonnaise
3	tablespoons GREY POUPON DIJON MUSTARD
½	cup sliced almonds
	Assorted crackers *or* bagel chips

In 1-quart casserole dish, stir together crabmeat, cream cheese, green onions, mayonnaise and mustard. Sprinkle with almonds. Bake at 350°F for 15 to 20 minutes or until heated through. Serve warm as dip with crackers or bagel chips.

Nutrition information per serving of dip: 166 calories, 15 g total fat (4 g saturated fat), 41 mg cholesterol, 330 mg sodium, 2 g carbohydrate, 1 g dietary fiber, 7 g protein.

Chicken Florentine

Makes 4 servings • Prep Time: 15 minutes • Cooking Time: 25 minutes

Delight family or friends with a special meal showcasing this zesty spinach-topped main dish, corn, sesame seed rolls and butterscotch brownies.

4	boneless, skinless chicken breast halves (about 1 pound)
1	tablespoon vegetable oil
1	(10-ounce) package frozen chopped spinach, thawed and drained
2	cloves garlic, crushed
1	cup milk
½	cup grated Parmesan cheese, divided
⅓	cup GREY POUPON DIJON MUSTARD

❶ In large skillet, over medium-high heat, lightly brown chicken on both sides in hot oil for 6 minutes. Transfer chicken to a 2-quart oblong baking dish.

❷ In same skillet, cook and stir spinach and garlic for 2 minutes. Stir in milk, ¼ cup Parmesan cheese and mustard; heat through. Pour spinach mixture over chicken. Sprinkle with remaining Parmesan cheese. Bake at 375°F for 15 to 20 minutes or until chicken is done.

Nutrition information per serving: 279 calories, 13 g total fat (5 g saturated fat), 74 mg cholesterol, 861 mg sodium, 8 g carbohydrate, 0 g dietary fiber, 32 g protein.

SWEET AND TANGY BARBECUED CHICKEN

Makes 6 servings • Prep Time: 15 minutes • Cooking Time: 1¼ hours

Team this lip-lickin'-good chicken with potato salad, steamed fresh green beans and icy cold glasses of lemonade.

1	medium onion, chopped
1	(8-ounce) can tomato sauce
½	cup cider vinegar
⅓	cup firmly packed light brown sugar
2	tablespoons GREY POUPON DIJON MUSTARD
1	teaspoon dried thyme leaves
6	chicken legs (drumstick and thigh attached)

❶ For sauce, in covered medium saucepan, over medium heat, cook onion in small amount of boiling water for 3 minutes or until tender; drain. Stir in tomato sauce, vinegar, brown sugar, mustard and thyme. Heat to a boil; reduce heat. Simmer, uncovered, for 15 minutes, stirring occasionally. Remove from heat.* Reserve 1 cup sauce for basting.

❷ Skin chicken, if desired. Rinse chicken; pat dry. Arrange chicken in 15½x10½x1-inch baking pan. Spoon remaining sauce over chicken.

❸ Bake at 375°F for 50 to 60 minutes or until chicken is done, basting occasionally with some of the reserved sauce. In small saucepan, heat any remaining sauce to a boil; spoon over chicken.

*Note: If you like, prepare the sauce ahead, then cover and store in refrigerator for up to 1 week.

Nutrition information per serving: 324 calories, 16 g total fat (4 g saturated fat), 105 mg cholesterol, 465 mg sodium, 14 g carbohydrate, 1 g dietary fiber, 30 g protein.

MUSHROOM CHICKEN IN WINE SAUCE

Mushroom Chicken in Wine Sauce*

Makes 4 servings • Prep Time: 20 minutes • Cooking Time: 35 minutes

For golden chicken, be sure the oil in the skillet is hot before you add the chicken pieces and leave room between the pieces so they'll brown rather than steam.

1	(2½- to 3-pound) broiler-fryer chicken, cut into 8 pieces
⅓	cup all-purpose flour
2	tablespoons vegetable oil
4	cups sliced fresh mushrooms
½	cup GREY POUPON DIJON *or* HONEY MUSTARD
½	cup dry white wine
2	tablespoons chopped fresh parsley

❶ Skin chicken, if desired. Rinse chicken; pat dry. Coat chicken with flour, shaking off excess. In large skillet, over medium-high heat, brown chicken in hot oil. Remove chicken from skillet.

❷ In same skillet, cook and stir mushrooms in pan drippings for 2 to 3 minutes or until tender. Stir in mustard and wine; return chicken to pan.

❸ Heat to a boil; reduce heat. Cover; simmer for 20 to 25 minutes or until chicken is done. Sprinkle with parsley.

Nutrition information per serving: 463 calories, 23 g total fat (5 g saturated fat), 99 mg cholesterol, 126 mg sodium,
23 g carbohydrate, 1 g dietary fiber, 33 g protein.

PESTO CHICKEN

Makes 4 servings • Prep Time: 10 minutes • Cooking Time: 20 minutes

*Create a festive party menu by starting with this easy main dish and adding
a bulgur-and-fruit pilaf, pull-apart rolls and baked apples.*

⅓ cup shredded mozzarella cheese (about 1½ ounces), divided
¼ cup purchased pesto sauce
¼ cup GREY POUPON DIJON MUSTARD
4 boneless, skinless chicken breast halves (about 1 pound)

❶ In small bowl, stir together ¼ cup mozzarella cheese, pesto sauce and mustard.

❷ Rinse chicken; pat dry. Place chicken in 13x9x2-inch baking dish. Spread mustard mixture evenly over chicken; top with remaining cheese. Bake at 350°F for 20 to 25 minutes or until done.

Nutrition information per serving: 276 calories, 16 g total fat (2 g saturated fat), 68 mg cholesterol, 597 mg sodium,
4 g carbohydrate, 0 g dietary fiber, 27 g protein.

Peppered Beef Tenderloin with Mushroom Sauce

Makes 6 servings • Prep Time: 10 minutes
Cooking Time: 20 minutes • Standing Time: 10 minutes

By serving this distinctive beef dish over hot cooked pasta, you'll be sure to savor every bit of the scrumptious stroganoff-like sauce. Featured in the menu on page 69.

4   tablespoons GREY POUPON DIJON MUSTARD, divided
1   teaspoon coarsely ground black pepper
1   (1½-pound) beef tenderloin
2   cups quartered fresh mushrooms
¾   cup beef broth, divided
1   cup light cream *or* half-and-half
2   tablespoons all-purpose flour

❶ In small bowl, combine 2 tablespoons mustard and pepper. Spread over surface of meat. Place meat on wire rack in shallow roasting pan. Insert meat thermometer in center of meat.

❷ Roast at 425°F to desired doneness, allowing 20 to 30 minutes for medium-rare (140°F) or 30 to 40 minutes for medium (155°F). Cover meat with foil to keep it warm and let stand for 10 minutes before carving. (The meat's temperature will rise 5° during standing.)

❸ Meanwhile, for sauce, in large skillet, cook mushrooms in ¼ cup beef broth until tender. In small bowl, stir together light cream or half-and-half, flour, remaining beef broth and remaining mustard; slowly stir into cooked mushrooms. Over medium-high heat, cook and stir until mixture thickens and begins to boil. Cook and stir for 1 minute more.

❹ To serve, thinly slice meat. Pass sauce to spoon over meat.

Nutrition information per serving: 239 calories, 13 g total fat (6 g saturated fat), 79 mg cholesterol, 415 mg sodium,
6 g carbohydrate, 0 g dietary fiber, 25 g protein.

MUSTARD-ORANGE LAMB CHOPS

MUSTARD-ORANGE LAMB CHOPS*

Makes 4 servings • Prep Time: 10 minutes • Cooking Time: 12 minutes

For juicy, tender lamb chops cooked to perfection, broil them only to medium doneness. The chops should still have a little pink in the center and be crusty brown on the outside. While the chops are broiling, prepare the sauce and some hot cooked orzo. Then, serve the chops over the orzo and spoon on the sauce.

⅓   cup orange marmalade *or* apricot preserves
3   tablespoons GREY POUPON DIJON MUSTARD
8   lamb rib chops, cut 1 inch thick, *or* 4 pork loin rib chops, cut ¾ inch thick
2   cups sliced fresh mushrooms
½   cup sliced green onions
1   tablespoon orange juice

❶ For glaze, in bowl, stir together marmalade or preserves and mustard. Reserve ⅓ cup glaze to use when preparing sauce.

❷ Broil lamb or pork chops 3 to 4 inches from heat source until done, turning and basting once with remaining glaze. Allow 7 to 11 minutes for lamb or 8 to 10 minutes for pork.

❸ Meanwhile, for sauce, spray medium saucepan with nonstick spray coating. Add mushrooms and green onions. Over medium heat, cook and stir for 3 to 4 minutes or until mushrooms are tender. Stir in orange juice and reserved glaze. Cook and stir until heated through. Spoon sauce over chops.

Nutrition information per serving: 295 calories, 12 g total fat (4 g saturated fat), 77 mg cholesterol, 361 mg sodium, 22 g carbohydrate, 2 g dietary fiber, 25 g protein.

LIME-MARINATED PORK CHOPS

**Makes 6 servings • Prep Time: 10 minutes • Marinating Time: 4 hours
Cooking Time: 45 minutes**

*Keep cleanup to a minimum by marinating the chops in a sealed plastic bag. Turn
the bag several times while refrigerating to help redistribute the marinade.*

6	boneless pork loin chops, cut 1¼ to 1½ inches thick
¼	cup GREY POUPON DIJON *or* HONEY MUSTARD
3	tablespoons lime juice
3	tablespoons Worcestershire sauce
2	tablespoons cider vinegar
1	tablespoon water

❶ Place pork chops in large glass baking dish. For marinade, in small bowl, combine mustard, lime juice, Worcestershire sauce, vinegar and water. Pour marinade over chops, turning chops to coat well. Cover; marinate in refrigerator for at least 4 hours or overnight, turning occasionally.

❷ Remove pork chops, reserving marinade. In small saucepan, heat reserved marinade to a boil. Cover; boil gently for 5 minutes. Set aside. In covered grill, arrange medium-hot coals around drip pan.* Place pork chops on grill rack over drip pan (not over coals); lower grill hood.

❸ Grill for 35 to 40 minutes or until done, turning once halfway through cooking and basting occasionally with some of the reserved marinade (add more coals to maintain heat as necessary). Discard any remaining marinade.

*Note: To broil pork chops in oven, broil 4 to 5 inches from heat source for 11 to 15 minutes or until done, turning once and basting occasionally with some of the reserved marinade.

Nutrition information per serving: 213 calories, 11 g total fat (4 g saturated fat), 77 mg cholesterol, 221 mg sodium,
2 g carbohydrate, 0 g dietary fiber, 25 g protein.

Spicy Mustard-Glazed Pork Ribs

Makes 4 servings • Prep Time: 10 minutes • Cooking Time: 1½ hours

*Complete your meal by serving coleslaw, sliced tomatoes and
chilled watermelon wedges with these meaty ribs.*

2½   to 3 pounds pork loin back ribs *or* spareribs
⅔   cup bottled sweet and sour sauce
⅓   cup GREY POUPON HONEY MUSTARD
2   tablespoons soy sauce
½   teaspoon five-spice powder (*or* ¼ teaspoon ground allspice *and* ¼ teaspoon ground cinnamon)

❶ Cut ribs into serving-size pieces. Place ribs, bone sides down, in shallow roasting pan. Bake at 350°F for 1 hour; drain. Meanwhile, for glaze, in small bowl, stir together sweet and sour sauce, mustard, soy sauce and spice. Reserve ½ cup glaze until serving time. Brush ribs with remaining glaze.

❷ Bake for 30 minutes more or until ribs are tender. In small saucepan, heat reserved glaze to a boil. Serve glaze with ribs.

Nutrition information per serving: 420 calories, 16 g total fat (6 g saturated fat), 81 mg cholesterol, 727 mg sodium,
25 g carbohydrate, 0 g dietary fiber, 40 g protein.

Penne with Sun-Dried Tomato Sauce

Makes 6 servings • Prep Time: 10 minutes • Cooking Time: 20 minutes

*If the sauce thickens too much before you have a chance to toss it with the hot pasta,
stir in a little extra light cream to make it the right consistency.*

1   pound penne pasta (about 5 cups)
½   cup sun-dried tomato strips in oil, drained
1   clove garlic, crushed
2   cups light cream *or* half-and-half
1   (10-ounce) package frozen peas, thawed
¼   cup GREY POUPON DIJON MUSTARD
1   tablespoon chopped fresh basil *or* 1 teaspoon dried basil leaves

❶ Cook pasta according to package directions; drain. Meanwhile, in medium saucepan, over medium heat, cook and stir sun-dried tomatoes and garlic for 2 minutes. Reduce heat to low.

❷ Stir in light cream or half-and-half, thawed peas, mustard and basil. Cook for 1 to 2 minutes or until sauce is heated through. Toss with hot cooked pasta to coat.

Nutrition information per serving: 461 calories, 13 g total fat (6 g saturated fat), 30 mg cholesterol, 347 mg sodium,
71 g carbohydrate, 2 g dietary fiber, 16 g protein.

COUNTRY DIJON SHRIMP SAUTÉ*

Makes 4 servings • Prep Time: 20 minutes • Cooking Time: 5 minutes

Serve these simple but elegant sautéed shrimp over fluffy hot cooked rice.

1	pound large fresh shrimp, peeled and deveined
1	clove garlic, crushed
3	tablespoons margarine *or* butter
¼	cup dry white wine
3	tablespoons GREY POUPON Country Dijon *or* DIJON MUSTARD

2 tablespoons chopped fresh parsley
Green and purple flowering kale, for garnish

❶ In large skillet, over medium-high heat, cook and stir shrimp and garlic in margarine or butter for 3 to 5 minutes or until shrimp are pink and done. Remove from heat.

COUNTRY DIJON SHRIMP SAUTÉ

MENU

COUNTRY DIJON SHRIMP SAUTÉ*

HOT COOKED RICE

MIXED GREENS SALAD WITH CREAMY
HONEY-JALAPEÑO DRESSING
(DRESSING RECIPE, PAGE 91)

FRENCH BREAD

CHOCOLATE TORTE

❷ Stir in wine and mustard. Return to heat; cook for 2 to 3
minutes more or until heated through. Remove from heat;
stir in parsley. Garnish with kale.

Nutrition information per serving: 165 calories, 9 g total fat (2 g saturated fat),
131 mg cholesterol, 522 mg sodium, 1 g carbohydrate, 0 g dietary fiber, 14 g protein.

GARLIC MASHED POTATOES

Makes 6 servings • Prep Time: 20 minutes • Cooking Time: 25 minutes

These garlicky potatoes are so flavorful, you won't need to add gravy.
Pictured on page 39 and featured in the menu on page 38.

- 2 pounds potatoes, peeled and cubed
- 1 medium onion, chopped
- 3 cloves garlic, coarsely chopped
- ¼ cup GREY POUPON DIJON MUSTARD
- ¼ cup margarine *or* butter, melted
- ¼ to ½ cup milk
- ¼ cup chopped fresh parsley

❶ In covered large saucepan, cook potatoes, onion and garlic in boiling water for 20 minutes or until potatoes are tender; drain.

❷ In large bowl, with electric mixer at medium speed, beat potato mixture until mashed. On low speed, gradually beat in mustard, melted margarine or butter and enough milk to make potatoes smooth and well blended. Stir in parsley.

Nutrition information per serving: 222 calories, 9 g total fat (2 g saturated fat), 1 mg cholesterol, 356 mg sodium, 33 g carbohydrate, 2 g dietary fiber, 4 g protein.

DIJON SCALLOPED POTATOES

Makes 4 servings • Prep Time: 15 minutes • Cooking Time: 1½ hours
Standing Time: 5 minutes

- 1 small onion, chopped
- 2 tablespoons margarine *or* butter
- 2 tablespoons all-purpose flour
- 1½ cups milk
- ½ cup GREY POUPON DIJON MUSTARD
- 4 medium baking potatoes (about 1½ pounds), peeled and thinly sliced
- ⅓ cup shredded Swiss cheese (about 1½ ounces)

❶ In medium saucepan, over medium heat, cook onion in margarine or butter until tender. Stir in flour; cook for 2 minutes. Slowly stir in milk. Cook and stir for 3 to 5 minutes more or until mixture thickens. Stir in mustard; heat through.

❷ In greased 2-quart casserole dish, alternately layer potatoes and mustard mixture. Cover; bake at 375°F for 1 hour. Sprinkle with cheese. Bake, uncovered, for 10 to 15 minutes more or until potatoes are tender and cheese is melted. Let stand for 5 minutes before serving.

Nutrition information per serving: 368 calories, 13 g total fat (4 g saturated fat), 16 mg cholesterol, 910 mg sodium, 51 g carbohydrate, 2 g dietary fiber, 13 g protein.

GRILLED VEGETABLES WITH HONEY DRESSING

Makes 6 servings • Prep Time: 20 minutes • Cooking Time: 6 minutes

If you can't locate miniature fresh mozzarella cheese balls, use 9 ounces of the larger balls and cut them into small pieces.

½ cup GREY POUPON HONEY MUSTARD
⅓ cup bottled Caesar salad dressing
1 medium eggplant, sliced
2 medium zucchini, sliced diagonally
1 medium yellow summer squash, sliced diagonally
1 (9-ounce) package miniature fresh mozzarella cheese balls, quartered
1 (7-ounce) jar roasted red bell peppers, drained and cut into thin matchstick strips

❶ For dressing, in small bowl, whisk together mustard and Caesar salad dressing. Reserve ½ cup dressing until serving time.

❷ Grill eggplant, zucchini and yellow squash over medium-high heat for 6 minutes or until tender, turning once and basting occasionally with remaining dressing.

❸ To serve, on large serving platter, arrange grilled vegetables. Top with cheese and roasted pepper strips. Drizzle with the ½ cup reserved dressing.

Nutrition information per serving: 270 calories, 17 g total fat (6 g saturated fat), 37 mg cholesterol, 200 mg sodium, 18 g carbohydrate, 3 g dietary fiber, 10 g protein.

THE BASICS

Add remarkable flavor to all types of foods with these spunky sauces, salad dressings, marinades, glazes and dips. Most of these simple recipes can be prepared in 10 minutes or less, and each will make the meal a standout, whether it's a last-minute weeknight supper or a carefully planned celebration dinner.

SAUCE DIJON À LA PROVENÇAL (RECIPE, PAGE 86)

Sauce Dijon à la Provençal

Makes about 2 cups (enough for 6 servings) • Prep Time: 5 minutes
Cooking Time: 30 minutes

Provençal refers to a style of cooking that's used in Provence, France, where ingredients such as tomatoes and onions are abundant and used in many dishes. Pictured on pages 84–85.

1	(14½-ounce) can stewed tomatoes, undrained
2	small onions, quartered
¼	cup GREY POUPON DIJON MUSTARD
1	teaspoon sugar

❶ In medium saucepan, over medium heat, heat tomatoes, onions, mustard and sugar to a boil; reduce heat. Cover; simmer for 25 minutes or until onions are tender, stirring occasionally.

❷ Serve warm sauce with chicken, beef, fish or pasta.

Nutrition information per serving of sauce: 41 calories, 1 g total fat (0 g saturated fat), 0 mg cholesterol, 467 mg sodium,
7 g carbohydrate, 0 g dietary fiber, 1 g protein.

Mustard-Chive Sauce

Makes about 1 cup (enough for 4 servings) • Prep Time: 5 minutes
Cooking Time: 5 minutes

Stirring the light cream or half-and-half into the flour with a wire whisk helps prevent lumps in this delicate sauce.

⅓	cup light cream *or* half-and-half
2	tablespoons all-purpose flour
¾	cup chicken broth
2	tablespoons chopped fresh chives
2	tablespoons GREY POUPON DIJON MUSTARD
¼	teaspoon coarsely ground black pepper

❶ In small saucepan, slowly whisk light cream or half-and-half into flour until smooth. Whisk in broth. Over medium heat, cook and stir until mixture thickens and begins to boil. Stir in chives, mustard and pepper. Cook and stir for 1 minute more.

❷ Serve warm sauce with poultry, beef, pork, lamb, sausage, fish or vegetables.

Nutrition information per serving of sauce: 56 calories, 3 g total fat (2 g saturated fat), 8 mg cholesterol, 343 mg sodium,
4 g carbohydrate, 0 g dietary fiber, 2 g protein.

Asian Glaze

Makes about ½ cup (enough for 4 servings) • Prep Time: 5 minutes

Brush on this ginger-flavored glaze only during the last few minutes of broiling, grilling or roasting so it doesn't scorch.

⅓   cup GREY POUPON HONEY MUSTARD
2   tablespoons firmly packed light brown sugar
2   tablespoons soy sauce
1   clove garlic, crushed
1   teaspoon ground ginger

❶ In small bowl, combine mustard, brown sugar, soy sauce, garlic and ginger.

❷ Use as a basting sauce for chicken, pork or seafood during the last 5 minutes of cooking.

Nutrition information per serving of glaze: 68 calories, 0 g total fat (0 g saturated fat), 0 mg cholesterol, 536 mg sodium, 15 g carbohydrate, 0 g dietary fiber, 1 g protein.

Orange-Mustard Glaze

Makes about ½ cup (enough for 4 servings) • Prep Time: 5 minutes

Only two ingredients are needed to make this super-speedy sauce.

¼   cup GREY POUPON DIJON *or* HONEY MUSTARD
¼   cup orange marmalade

❶ In small bowl, combine mustard and orange marmalade.

❷ Use as a basting sauce for chicken, pork or ham during the last 5 minutes of cooking.

Nutrition information per serving of glaze: 70 calories, 1 g total fat (0 g saturated fat), 0 mg cholesterol, 381 mg sodium, 15 g carbohydrate, 1 g dietary fiber, 1 g protein.

HERB-MUSTARD RUB

Makes about ⅓ cup (enough for 4 to 6 servings) • Prep Time: 10 minutes

This simple blend of flavors makes a wonderful, golden coating for roasted poultry or meat.

1	small onion, finely chopped
2	tablespoons GREY POUPON DIJON *or* Country Dijon Mustard
¼	teaspoon dried basil leaves
¼	teaspoon dried thyme leaves
¼	teaspoon ground black pepper

❶ In small bowl, combine onion, mustard, basil, thyme and pepper.

❷ Spread on raw poultry, beef, pork or lamb before cooking.

Nutrition information per serving of marinade: 14 calories, 0 g total fat (0 g saturated fat), 0 mg cholesterol, 189 mg sodium, 1 g carbohydrate, 0 g dietary fiber, 1 g protein.

ITALIAN MUSTARD MARINADE

Makes about ⅔ cup (enough for 6 servings) • Prep Time: 5 minutes

When using this robust marinade, refrigerate chicken or pork for 2 to 24 hours and seafood for 30 minutes to 2 hours.

⅓	cup GREY POUPON DIJON MUSTARD
⅓	cup bottled Italian salad dressing

❶ In small bowl, whisk together mustard and Italian salad dressing.

❷ Use as a marinade for chicken, pork or seafood.

Nutrition information per serving of marinade: 78 calories, 7 g total fat (1 g saturated fat), 0 mg cholesterol, 436 mg sodium, 2 g carbohydrate, 0 g dietary fiber, 1 g protein.

LEMON-BASIL MARINADE

Makes about ⅔ cup (enough for 6 servings) • **Prep Time: 5 minutes**

To make the chicken breasts on the cover, refrigerate them in this full-flavored citrus marinade for 2 to 24 hours. Then, remove the chicken pieces from the marinade and broil them 4 to 6 inches from heat source for 10 to 15 minutes or until chicken is done, turning once. Pictured on cover.

⅓ cup cider vinegar
¼ cup GREY POUPON DIJON *or* Country Dijon Mustard
2   tablespoons vegetable oil
2   to 3 teaspoons dried basil leaves
1   teaspoon grated lemon peel
1   clove garlic, crushed

❶ In small bowl, whisk together vinegar, mustard, oil, basil, lemon peel and garlic.

❷ Use as a marinade for chicken, pork or seafood.

Nutrition information per serving of marinade: 54 calories, 5 g total fat (1 g saturated fat), 0 mg cholesterol, 252 mg sodium, 2 g carbohydrate, 0 g dietary fiber, 1 g protein.

WINE-AND-HERB MARINADE

Makes about 1 cup (enough for 6 to 8 servings) • **Prep Time: 10 minutes**

Use this flavorful mixture to marinate cubes of meat. Then, thread the cubes on skewers with bell pepper pieces and whole mushrooms to make kabobs.

½ cup dry red wine
¼ cup GREY POUPON DIJON *or* Country Dijon Mustard
2   tablespoons lemon juice
1   tablespoon chopped fresh rosemary *or* ¾ teaspoon dried rosemary leaves
1   tablespoon chopped fresh marjoram *or* ¾ teaspoon dried marjoram leaves
1   tablespoon olive oil *or* vegetable oil
1   teaspoon coarsely ground black pepper

❶ In small bowl, combine wine, mustard, lemon juice, rosemary, marjoram, oil and pepper.

❷ Use as a marinade for beef, pork or lamb.

Nutrition information per serving of marinade: 49 calories, 3 g total fat (0 g saturated fat), 0 mg cholesterol, 265 mg sodium, 2 g carbohydrate, 0 g dietary fiber, 1 g protein.

Poppy Seed Dijon Vinaigrette

Makes about 1¼ cups (enough for 10 servings) • Prep Time: 5 minutes

This orange-flavored dressing tastes terrific with a variety of fresh fruits and greens. Strawberries, cantaloupe and kiwifruit combined with mixed salad greens or spinach is an especially good combination.

½   cup orange juice
⅓   cup red *or* white wine vinegar
¼   cup GREY POUPON DIJON MUSTARD
2   tablespoons olive oil
1   tablespoon poppy seed

❶ In small bowl, whisk together orange juice, vinegar, mustard, oil and poppy seed.

❷ Serve immediately or cover and store in refrigerator for up to 1 week. Use as a dressing for salad greens.

Nutrition information per serving of dressing: 41 calories, 3 g total fat (0 g saturated fat), 0 mg cholesterol, 152 mg sodium, 2 g carbohydrate, 0 g dietary fiber, 1 g protein.

Poppy Seed Dijon Vinaigrette

Creamy Honey-Jalapeño Dressing

Makes about ¾ cup (enough for 6 servings) • Prep Time: 8 minutes

Because jalapeño peppers contain oils that can burn your skin and eyes, wear plastic gloves (or cover your hands with plastic bags) whenever working with these peppers. Featured in the menu on page 81.

½ cup dairy sour cream
3 tablespoons GREY POUPON HONEY MUSTARD
2 tablespoons milk
1 tablespoon seeded and chopped jalapeño pepper
1 tablespoon lime juice *or* lemon juice
¼ teaspoon paprika

❶ In electric blender or food processor, combine all ingredients. Blend until smooth.

❷ Serve immediately or cover and store in refrigerator for up to 1 week. Use as a dressing for salad greens.

Nutrition information per serving of dressing: 60 calories, 4 g total fat (3 g saturated fat), 9 mg cholesterol, 20 mg sodium, 4 g carbohydrate, 0 g dietary fiber, 1 g protein.

Classic Dijon Vinaigrette

Makes about 2 cups (enough for 16 servings) • Prep Time: 5 minutes

Keep this zesty dressing on hand for all occasions. Pictured on pages 4–5.

1¼ cups vegetable oil *or* olive oil
⅓ cup GREY POUPON DIJON MUSTARD
⅓ cup red wine vinegar
¼ teaspoon ground black pepper

In bowl, whisk together oil, mustard, vinegar and pepper. Serve immediately or cover and store in refrigerator for up to 1 week. Use as a dressing for salad greens.

Nutrition information per serving of dressing: 157 calories, 17 g total fat (2 g saturated fat), 0 mg cholesterol, 126 mg sodium, 1 g carbohydrate, 0 g dietary fiber, 0 g protein.

Citrus Dressing

Makes about 1 cup (enough for 8 servings) • Prep Time: 5 minutes

Pictured on page 16 and featured in the menu on page 17.

⅓ cup honey
⅓ cup orange juice
¼ cup GREY POUPON DIJON MUSTARD

In small bowl, whisk together honey, orange juice and mustard. Serve immediately or cover and store in refrigerator for up to 1 week. Use as a dressing for salad greens.

Nutrition information per serving of dressing: 57 calories, 0 g total fat (0 g saturated fat), 0 mg cholesterol, 190 mg sodium, 13 g carbohydrate, 0 g dietary fiber, 1 g protein.

Cracked Pepper Dijon Dressing

Makes about 1 cup (enough for 8 servings) • Prep Time: 5 minutes

⅓ cup dairy sour cream
⅓ cup GREY POUPON DIJON MUSTARD
⅓ cup buttermilk *or* whole milk
1 tablespoon sugar
½ to 1 teaspoon coarsely cracked black pepper
¼ teaspoon garlic powder

In bowl, blend all ingredients. Serve immediately or cover and store in refrigerator for up to 1 week. Use as a dressing for salad greens or as a dip with vegetables.

Nutrition information per serving of dressing: 44 calories, 3 g total fat (1 g saturated fat), 5 mg cholesterol, 268 mg sodium, 3 g carbohydrate, 0 g dietary fiber, 1 g protein.

BACON-HORSERADISH DIP

Makes about 1½ cups (enough for 8 appetizer servings) • Prep Time: 10 minutes
Cooking Time: 5 minutes

The smoky bacon gives this dip a down-home cookout flavor.

1 cup mayonnaise
½ cup GREY POUPON DIJON *or* Country Dijon Mustard
4 slices bacon, cooked and crumbled
1 tablespoon prepared horseradish
   Assorted cut-up vegetables

❶ In small bowl, combine mayonnaise, mustard, bacon and horseradish until well blended. Cover; refrigerate until serving time.

❷ Serve as a dip with assorted cut-up vegetables.

Nutrition information per serving of dip: 236 calories, 25 g total fat (4 g saturated fat), 19 mg cholesterol, 606 mg sodium,
2 g carbohydrate, 0 g dietary fiber, 2 g protein.

MUSTARD-AND-BEER CHEESE DIP

Makes about 3 cups (enough for 16 appetizer servings) • Prep Time: 10 minutes
Cooking Time: 10 minutes

Besides using pretzels, you can scoop up bits of this well-seasoned dip with broccoli or cauliflower flowerettes,
cubed rye bread or bite-size pieces of cooked, small red potatoes. Featured in the menu on page 43.

12 ounces pasteurized processed cheese spread, cubed
 4 ounces cream cheese, cubed
⅔ cup beer
½ cup GREY POUPON DIJON MUSTARD
⅓ cup chopped green onions
    Chopped red bell pepper, for garnish
    Soft pretzels, warmed

❶ In medium saucepan, over low heat, heat cheese spread and cream cheese until melted and smooth, stirring occasionally. Slowly blend in beer and mustard. Stir in green onions.

❷ Pour into serving bowl. Garnish with bell pepper. Serve as a dip with pretzels.

Nutrition information per serving of dip: 100 calories, 7 g total fat (4 g saturated fat), 20 mg cholesterol, 496 mg sodium,
3 g carbohydrate, 0 g dietary fiber, 5 g protein.

RECIPE INDEX

Nutrition Information

*So you can keep track of what you eat,
each recipe in this book lists nutritional values
for one serving. Here's how we made our
analyses: When a recipe gives a choice of
ingredients (such as margarine or butter), we
use the first choice in our analysis. Ingredients
listed as optional or for garnish were omitted
from our calculations. Finally, all values were
rounded to the nearest whole number.*

Metric Cooking Hints

By making a few conversions, cooks in Australia, Canada, and the United Kingdom can use the recipes in *Meals Made Easy with Grey Poupon Mustard*. The charts on this page provide a guide for converting measurements from the U.S. customary system, which is used throughout this book, to the imperial and metric systems. There also is a conversion table for oven temperatures to accommodate the differences in oven calibrations.

Product Differences: Most of the ingredients called for in the recipes in this book are available in English-speaking countries. However, some are known by different names. Here are some common American ingredients and their possible counterparts:

■ Sugar is granulated or castor sugar.
■ Powdered sugar is icing sugar.
■ All-purpose flour is plain household flour or white flour. When self-rising flour is used in place of all-purpose flour in a recipe that calls for leavening, omit the leavening agent (baking soda or baking powder) and salt.
■ Light-colored corn syrup is golden syrup.
■ Cornstarch is cornflour.
■ Baking soda is bicarbonate of soda.
■ Vanilla is vanilla essence.
■ Green, red, or yellow sweet peppers are capsicums.
■ Golden raisins are sultanas.

Volume and Weight: Americans traditionally use cup measures for liquid and solid ingredients. The chart, below, shows the approximate imperial and metric equivalents. If you are accustomed to weighing solid ingredients, the following approximate equivalents will be helpful.

■ 1 cup butter, castor sugar, or rice = 8 ounces = about 250 grams
■ 1 cup flour = 4 ounces = about 125 grams
■ 1 cup icing sugar = 5 ounces = about 150 grams

Spoon measures are used for smaller amounts of ingredients. Although the size of the tablespoon varies slightly in different countries, for practical purposes and for recipes in this book, a straight substitution is all that's necessary.

Measurements made using cups or spoons always should be level unless stated otherwise.

Equivalents: U.S. = Australia/U.K.

⅛ teaspoon = 0.5 ml
¼ teaspoon = 1 ml
½ teaspoon = 2 ml
1 teaspoon = 5 ml
1 tablespoon = 1 tablespoon
¼ cup = 2 tablespoons = 2 fluid ounces = 60 ml
⅓ cup = ¼ cup = 3 fluid ounces = 90 ml
½ cup = ⅓ cup = 4 fluid ounces = 120 ml

⅔ cup = ½ cup = 5 fluid ounces = 150 ml
¾ cup = ⅔ cup = 6 fluid ounces = 180 ml
1 cup = ¾ cup = 8 fluid ounces = 240 ml
1¼ cups = 1 cup
2 cups = 1 pint
1 quart = 1 litre
½ inch = 1.27 cm
1 inch = 2.54 cm

Baking Pan Sizes

American	Metric
8x1½-inch round baking pan	20x4-centimetre cake tin
9x1½-inch round baking pan	23x3.5-centimetre cake tin
11x7x1½-inch baking pan	28x18x4-centimetre baking tin
13x9x2-inch baking pan	30x20x3-centimetre baking tin
2-quart rectangular baking dish	30x20x3-centimetre baking tin
15x10x1-inch baking pan	30x25x2-centimetre baking tin (Swiss roll tin)
9-inch pie plate	22x4- or 23x4-centimetre pie plate
7- or 8-inch springform pan	18- or 20-centimetre springform or loose-bottom cake tin
9x5x3-inch loaf pan	23x13x7-centimetre or 2-pound narrow loaf tin or paté tin
1½-quart casserole	1.5-litre casserole
2-quart casserole	2-litre casserole

Oven Temperature Equivalents

Fahrenheit Setting	Celsius Setting*	Gas Setting
300°F	150°C	Gas Mark 2 (slow)
325°F	160°C	Gas Mark 3 (moderately slow)
350°F	180°C	Gas Mark 4 (moderate)
375°F	190°C	Gas Mark 5 (moderately hot)
400°F	200°C	Gas Mark 6 (hot)
425°F	220°C	Gas Mark 7
450°F	230°C	Gas Mark 8 (very hot)
Broil		Grill

* Electric and gas ovens may be calibrated using Celsius. However, for an electric oven, increase the Celsius setting 10 to 20 degrees when cooking above 160°C. For convection or forced-air ovens (gas or electric), lower the temperature setting 10°C when cooking at all heat levels.